LEADING
gracefully

LEADING
gracefully

A WOMAN'S GUIDE TO CONFIDENT, AUTHENTIC & EFFECTIVE LEADERSHIP

MONIQUE SVAZLIAN TALLON

HIGHEST PATH
PUBLISHING

www.leadinggracefullybook.com

First Edition
ISBN: 978-0-9969844-0-9

Cover Design by Sarah Knouse
Typeset by Wildwood Publishing

14 13 12 11 10 / 10 9 8 7 6 5 4 3 2 1

To my loving husband Chris
&
my great-grandmother Maritza

Contents

Introduction

I was born a first-generation American to Armenian parents, raised in a traditional and conservative household, and at the same time grew up in the most progressive and liberal of cities, San Francisco. My parents sent me to an all-girls Catholic high school thinking that was the safest route, and they wouldn't let me date till I was in college. I spent most of my early twenties rebelling against them, stuck in an identity crisis and had to really dig deep to figure out who I was at my core.

By my mid-twenties I found myself working in the corporate world, leading large-scale conferences and events. I landed a job at a well-known technology company in the very male-dominated Silicon Valley. However, this company's head was a female CEO and I had the opportunity to witness her lead the organization to great success. And I was—a young, twenty something manager, working my way up the ladder, with high hopes and ambitions.

But as I stepped into leadership positions, I had a hard time finding women role models that I really connected to. I also

1

had a hard time getting noticed for promotions. I saw others move up the proverbial ladder, while I just kept my head down and busted my butt to no avail. There was something wrong with this picture. I quickly realized that getting ahead wasn't necessarily based only on merit. It was based on visibility and building relationships with those in decision-making roles. Unfortunately, at the time, this wasn't my strong suit! To top it all off, I worked for a female boss who was more interested in taking most of the credit for my efforts. When she suddenly resigned, I decided this was my chance to prove myself and gain visibility. So I bravely volunteered to take over her role, which entailed producing a 10,000-person conference for our customers.

As the reality of what I had volunteered for began to sink in, I realized that although I had managed many large events before, I had never done anything on this scale. I was now responsible for the largest, most high profile consumer-facing event for our company. I had to figure out a game plan and step into my leadership, fast. But first I had another big decision to make—*how was I going to show up as a leader?* Was I going to emulate my female ex-boss and continue micromanaging my teams? Or was I going to find another style that would work better and felt more authentic to me?

I soon realized there was NO way I could micro-manage as my previous boss had successfully done because (a) it just wasn't who I was and (b) I didn't know *what* to delegate because I had never done this before! The only option I had was to ask my team to help me tackle this monster project. So on the first day of our big task force meeting with 20 executives staring at little old me, I started the meeting by openly admitting that I had no idea what I was doing. "I need your help!" I declared. "I've never managed an event this size, and I know some of you have been involved with the planning of this conference in the past, so I really need all of you to help me produce the best conference ever!"

I thought for sure I had completely lost my credibility and authority in that moment. I never dreamed that being so vulnerable would have the impact that it did. What happened next was nothing short of miraculous.

One by one, people took on roles and responsibilities based on their past experience and department expertise. Each person on the team came forward to help, and from then on, they continued to come to our task force meetings prepared and ready to share and contribute. Instead of me having to tell people what to do, they took ownership of their respective tasks, and came to me with their knowledge and expertise. In short, everyone stepped up to the plate and contributed all that they could to make our conference a success.

My Learning

What I discovered from this experience was that by getting out of the way and empowering people to take responsibility, I created an environment where collaboration and creativity flourished. I didn't have to micro-manage everything because they were naturally creative, resourceful, and accountable. The more I trusted them, the more they delivered. By being totally vulnerable, admitting I didn't have all the answers and by asking for help, I had connected with them at that first meeting on a very human level and established immediate trust. From that point forward, they were dedicated to helping me by being contributing members of the team. Which was lucky for me, because that is exactly what I needed to produce this gigantic event!

But that's not all that I did differently. I also spent time establishing relationships with key players, really taking the time to work with them to get to know them. I opened up channels of communication and empowered them to make decisions so they could work amongst themselves without me becoming the bottleneck. I communicated my strong vision for the event, and what I hoped people would experience and take away from the conference, inspiring our teams with a compelling vision of the best-run event our community had ever experienced. And I also delegated, setting clear expectations and creating accountability for all of my teams. Of course there were moments where I wanted to jump off a cliff, but for the most part I was able to keep calm and stay focused.

The results were surprising. "Working with you is such a breath of fresh air," my team members would tell me. At the conference, we got comments from attendees saying how much they felt cared for and how well organized the event was. "This is one of the best events we have ever attended." What they didn't know was our success was due to the collaborative effort of hundreds of people behind the scenes that worked together to pull it off, under my direction. Needless to say, I was very proud of our collective accomplishment.

Women Can Make a Different Choice

This huge learning experience taught me that women (and men) have a choice on how they show up in their leadership. Outdated, more masculine styles of command & control, authority, and hierarchical structures can sometimes be necessary, but not always. And more and more, these approaches no longer work in our fast-changing world. In 2015, Millennials have now become the majority of the workforce. They are looking for flatter structures, more autonomy, purpose and work/life flexibility in the companies they work for. If organizations want to attract and retain the best talent, they need to listen deeply to these requests, instead of feeling threatened by them. In an ever-increasing competitive environment, businesses, want to drive innovation and creativity to stay ahead of the curve. In order to thrive, they need to create inclusive cultures by leveraging diversity. This means cultivating leaders who encourage people to contribute, be creative, and thrive.

All of this requires us to collectively redefine what leadership looks like. It requires a more integrated, balanced approach where feminine qualities of leadership are brought into the mix and valued. But for far too long, women have been told and taught that bringing their feminine selves to work is not OK. Many of us have given up some of our natural strengths just to "fit in" with our male counterparts. Isn't it time to examine if this has really served us, and think about whether we need to find a different approach, which includes all parts of ourselves—both masculine and feminine? And isn't it time that we give men the permission to integrate feminine qualities in how they show up as leaders?

Realizing that I had an alternative choice in my style as a female leader was life changing for me. It gave me a sense of hope knowing that I could be true to myself, be taken seriously and still do a good job. It helped me gain confidence in my abilities and gave me a sense of ease, knowing I didn't have to pretend to be someone I wasn't. It showed me that women could be effective, if not more effective, when they practice Feminine Leadership, by bringing more parts of their authentic self to the table.

Emerging women leaders are hungry for powerful yet authentic and feminine role models to show them the way. Yet they're looking around and not finding them. Instead, they find women who seem to be either threatened by them, or feel the need to compete due to generational biases. This more masculine style of leadership feels outdated and less authentic to the current generation of women in the workplace. If we are to truly thrive, close the gender gap, and lead the way as change makers, we must find another path to work together through generational lines and support each other along the way. Most importantly, we need to adapt to a changing competitive landscape that is asking their leaders to be more inclusive and collaborative. This book provides the pathway to do just that.

CHAPTER 1
The Current State of Affairs

It's a Man's World

Since women entered the workplace, they have had to navigate a man's world. At first, women decided they would do this by literally looking like men. "I remember when I first entered the workplace, I cut my hair short, wore a dark suit and a little tie, so I wouldn't stick out," says Diane Reichenberger who is Head of Strategy at a Fortune 500 Company. She goes on to describe how afraid she was to be feminine in any way. "I didn't want anyone thinking I wasn't capable, so I did what I could to fit in. Finally, as a senior executive, I feel free enough to embrace my femininity."

This is the story of countless women who were the pioneers of the feminist movement, the courageous women who braved ridicule, harassment, and all sorts of *Mad Men*-esque behavior to pave the way for the rest of us. In those days, you had to look like a man, act like a man, and practically *be* a man to be taken seriously in business. And it worked for those women who were willing to play the part.

What it also did was slowly lead to the masculinization of women. As women took on more responsibilities once held by men, they felt the need to do it the same way men did. They adopted and conformed to masculine qualities they were observing around them, taking on traditional forms of leadership such as command and control, or authoritative styles of leadership that could be described as aggressive, competitive, and dominating. While this might have been effective and allowed women to "prove" that they could lead just as well as men could, it also had a detrimental effect on their identity, self-esteem, self-worth and also on their relationship to the feminine. Most of all, women ended up believing that showing any type of weakness was bad, and would hurt their career advancement. They began to compensate by acting as strong and as tough as men.

It's worth noting the tremendous effort, courage, and bravery of the women in the first and second wave of the feminist movement of the 60s, 70s and beyond, paving the way for us to have the opportunities we have today. With their heads held high, brave and strong women like Susan B. Anthony, Gloria Steinem, and Betty Friedan walked into the fire, day after day, to prove women's worth and to fight the political battles that won the legislative protection and rights women enjoy today in the United States. For that, I and millions of other women will be forever grateful.

Yet since that time, women have evolved to operate in a man's world. Adapting to fit in a corporate world really designed for men, by men, it resulted in the swinging of the pendulum from one extreme to another. It took women from a state of being overly feminine (and not empowered) to a state of over-masculinization. The result—women decided to leave their strengths at home. They started to hide their emotions, stopped trusting their intuition, and began acting like "ice queens" or Queen Bees in the workplace to conform and compete in the boy's club. They took on more of a command-and-control style of leadership, not because they wanted to, but because it was what they saw being role-modeled around them by men. Not only did this lead to unintended negative consequences on women's self-expression, but it's also had unintended consequences in their effectiveness as leaders in business and in the world.

As women gave up more and more parts of themselves, they also stopped expressing their unique gifts and talents. Instead of speaking up, voicing their opinions, and making decisions, they gave up their power, deferring to their male counterparts or compensated and ruled with an iron fist. They underestimated their full potential, allowing themselves to fall victim to a male-centric, patriarchal model that promotes self-interest, separation, maximization of profits, and infinite expansion of economies. While busy trying to "be successful" and "advance" in this paradigm, women have compromised an essential part of who they are, along with their voice, gifts, and talents.

As Arianna Huffington has said, we are currently in the third women's revolution, and our job is to take that work one step further, to redefine what feminism and the word 'feminine' really mean and explore what it looks like to be an authentic woman in the world and in the workplace, cultivating and expressing all parts of our true essence. We can do this by reintegrating those elements of ourselves, remembering and valuing our true gifts. We can do this by inviting men to join us as collaborators and partners, to help them reclaim the feminine within themselves. Most importantly, we can do this by healing the wounding we carry from eons of persecution. Only by doing these things can we collectively begin swinging the pendulum back towards balance.

The Time for Women Is Now

The timing for women to reclaim their true power and step into their leadership couldn't be better. In his recent career advice to women, Warren Buffet said, "We've seen what can be accomplished when we use 50% of our human capacity. If you visualize what 100% can do, you'll join me as an unbridled optimist about America's future." If that's not a call to action, I don't know what is!

My belief is that women aren't holding 50% of leadership positions in the world because they have not yet found a real balance in their leadership style partly due to the mixed messages they receive. "Lean in, be more ambitious, speak up, ask for a raise, be more assertive." As many of you have probably experienced, you're damned if you do and damned if you don't. If you do any of those things, you put yourself at risk of being labeled "bitchy" or "bossy." If you don't take the advice, you're seen as a doormat, not leader-like, and given all of the office work to do, instead of being seen as a real player. The bottom line is that all of this is a symptom of a larger problem that is sometimes hard to pinpoint. The fact is that women are still trying to get ahead in a man's world, and unfortunately are forced to adapt to the unconscious biases and gender stereotypes that go along with that.

This has often been referred to as "The Tightrope"—walking a fine line between being too masculine and too feminine in your leadership approach at work. While we often assume that men are masculine and women are feminine, the truth is that those two things are independent of biological sex. Men can take on feminine qualities just as easily as women can take on masculine characteristics. And here is where I'd like to make a clear distinction—when I speak about feminine and masculine, I am referring to the *qualities* invoked when we think of those words, not gender in the traditional sense of man and woman. In this book, I associate the word 'feminine' to qualities like vulnerability, empathy, humility, openness, and collaboration. In contrast, I define 'masculine' traits as qualities like being logical, assertive, daring, decisive and resilient.

What I am not suggesting is that women conform to what we unfortunately tend to think of as feminine—that is, to be weak, meek, indecisive, subordinate or overly sensitive. Rather we can begin to redefine what it is to be a leader in the 21st century, by recognizing that women (and men) have an untapped resource of empowered feminine qualities that can be used as strengths. By combining these with more traditional masculine qualities, women can leverage their strengths to become better leaders. The real challenge is how to walk the tightrope and balance these seemingly contrasting qualities in our leadership— how to stay open and receptive while being decisive, or how to be assertive while practicing humility, to ensure we are liked and accepted by our peers and still be effective.

The Current Leadership Landscape

So why should we care about this? The main reason is that there is still a huge gap of women in leadership positions: women still lead only 14% of top executive positions in the Fortune 500. And only 21 of the CEOs of those companies are women. If we look at that statistic from another perspective that means 86% of top executive positions of Fortune 500s are held by men and 476 out of 500 CEOs are also men. We can see the same discouraging statistics in politics. Of 197 heads of state, only 22 are women. In national politics, women hold just 19% of congressional offices. For women of color, the figures are even lower, making only 6.2% of the total 535 members of Congress. And when it comes to wages, we still see a considerable difference. In 2014, women made 79 cents for every dollar earned by men, a gender wage gap of 21%, according to the Institute of Women's Policy Research. Given that we make up over 50% of the professional work force, these numbers tell us something isn't working.

As discouraging as those numbers may be, there are also plenty of encouraging ones showing us the importance of having women in power. Statistics show us that when women are in the boardroom, they make better decisions that lead to better financial performance. On average, companies with the highest percentages of women board of directors outperformed those with the least by 66%.

More importantly, studies have also shown that women corporate directors are significantly more inclined to make decisions by taking the interests of multiple stakeholders into account in order to arrive at a fair and moral decision. They will also tend to use cooperation, collaboration, and consensusbuilding more often—and more effectively—in order to make sound decisions. It's also no surprise that social enterprises are far more likely to be started by women than mainstream businesses, with 38% of social enterprises being led by women. There are even studies that show that men are more compassionate and generous when there is a woman present.

Having more women at the top is not only good for business, it's good for everyone involved, including the planet. And that's why addressing women's advancement in leadership positions is a pivotal issue of our time. It's also the biggest economic opportunity of the 21st century. With women making up over 60% of the educated talent pool as well as 80% of decision-making consumers, business cannot ignore the fact that including women in executive positions is essential if they want to appeal to this mass market and make sure they are getting the best talent on board. So when we advocate for gender equality in the workplace, or think about closing the gender gap, we need to look at the data and refer back to the real business case that exists for having more women in leadership positions.

But here's the thing—it's not just about having any type of woman at the top. There are too many stories of women leaders of big companies who have quickly risen to great heights, but have then come tumbling down just as quickly (if not more quickly). Take Carly Fiorina, former CEO of Hewlett-Packard. During her six-year tenure as Chief Executive Officer of HP, the company's stock to drop by 50%, losing close to one billion dollars in earnings. According to a top tech CEO, "she was a value destruction machine with near zero cultural sensitivity," which created a culture of fear and division within the company. Although her intentions may have been good, her leadership approach proved to be ineffective and led to poor business results. It begs the question, what might have been different if Ms. Fiorina embodied a few feminine qualities such as vulnerability or more empathy toward her stakeholders? Might she have been a better leader, alienated fewer people, or still be in the job today?

The point here is that it's not just about getting to the top— it's about how women lead once they do get to the top and how they might do better if they adopted a more balanced approach style across the board. For senior female executives, this might be a radical idea, and not one that is easy to adopt for some. If this is you, my invitation is to consider the idea that you can be more effective if you use a radically different approach—one that is more balanced and more aligned with your strengths and abilities. For women who are mid-career or just starting out— my suggestion is that perhaps this approach will not only help you increase your confidence, raise your visibility and effectiveness, but also keep you engaged and motivated through using a model of leadership that feels more authentic. My hope is that through offering a new roadmap, it will keep women climbing the ladder instead of opting out, which can get us all one step closer to closing the gender gap.

The New Story

When we look around, we begin to see that the male-centric model is beginning to fall apart. A world of infinite expansion and maximization of profit is unsustainable. It's proving ineffective and is actually now threatening our entire civilization. Take the global economic meltdown of 2008, for example. Huge companies like AIG and Lehman Brothers collapsed overnight due to shady financial dealings that nearly brought down the world's financial markets. Or how about the negligent use of our planet's resources, which have created unsustainable practices that are threatening our very existence, which most of the world's scientists have agreed are the leading cause of climate change? Or the endless wars that are now creating a migrant crisis seen since World War II? Everywhere we look, we see the effects of our global value system that is built on concepts of expansion, profit and inequality. We cannot keep up the game for much longer. As one of my teachers and foremost thinkers and authors of our time, Charles Eisenstein, says, "It is time to step out of the old story and into the new one, into a more beautiful world our hearts know is possible."

One radical and visionary solution this book explores is one very different than most other books on this subject offer. *If women want to become leaders and make an impact in the world, they must first reclaim their feminine power and learn to balance it with the current masculine paradigm.* No longer can women afford to conform and adapt to fit into a world dominated by male-centric values. The corporate landscape is craving a rebalancing where feminine values are equally represented, driving business decisions and affecting the way we form our cultures. There is much more at stake than ever before. So how can we do this? How can women reclaim their power and find true balance?

The purpose of this book is to explore this topic in more depth, through offering guidance and sharing my personal experiences, as well as highlighting examples of other women who currently embody authentic feminine expression and balanced leadership in various sectors, from business to politics, from media to non-profits. This book is meant to inspire anyone who has a vision for a more just and equal world for all of earth's inhabitants, for anyone who has an urge to make a difference, to lead in a way that brings about lasting transformation within yourself, your communities, and the world.

Introducing the Feminine Leadership Model™

Through personal experience, research, interviewing women leaders and entrepreneurs and many years running Highest Path Consulting (an international executive coaching and training company focused on diversity and inclusion), as well as running women's workshops and conferences, I've developed a model for leadership that I think can be transformative if adopted and integrated with traditional approaches to leadership. I call it the Feminine Leadership Model™ or FLM as I'll call it from here on out. Although the skills in this model transcend gender, as they are universal, some of them do tend to have a more 'feminine' quality to them, and that is the reason I have chosen to name it thus. Both women *and* men can benefit from these skills, and they aren't qualities that I've just picked randomly; McKinsey has identified many of these skills to positively impact organizational performance.

FEMININE LEADERSHIP MODEL™

This model features 7 Feminine Strengths and 4 Masculine Traits that can help women find the right balance as they walk the tightrope of leadership. When women are grounded in their power, they are Centered and able to fully incorporate the feminine strengths of Vision, Vulnerability, Care, Intuition, Empathy, Collaboration, and Humility. They are also able to bring in more traditional, masculine leadership traits such as being Daring, Decisive, Resilient, and Assertive when the situation calls for it. This in turn makes them leaders that inspire collaboration and innovation on the teams they manage and the businesses they run. The FLM represents a dance between the masculine and feminine, and gives us a roadmap to walk the tightrope as we choose when to use the qualities that give us our desired impact. As each situation is different and requires a different approach, you will learn how to incorporate these qualities in a way that lets you lead confidently, authentically and gracefully.

When women lead gracefully, they are able to encourage their teams and businesses to be much more inclusive, where people feel like their ideas matter, where their input is valued, and where people feel acknowledged for their contributions. This in turn leads to an atmosphere that can give birth to innovative ideas, ultimately leading to better business. But I would be doing myself a disservice if I told you that better business was the only reason that the Feminine Leadership approach is important. It is also important because when women are fully empowered, their voices and opinions are heard. When women make decisions, they take others into consideration, including our communities and our planet, not just the bottom line. And that is the kind of business we need to be running in the 21st century, one that equally represents the values and interests held by women.

Since women are facing a unique challenge and have an opportunity to shift the leadership landscape, the exercises and advice in this book are geared for women's development specifically. That is not to say that men cannot and should not also adopt and utilize these 21st century leadership strengths, and I do encourage you to share this model with them. In fact, I would venture to say many men, including current US President Barack Obama, embody both masculine and feminine qualities. My belief is that over time, this will be the leadership model that everyone will embody, regardless of gender.

I also understand that some women might have an aversion to the term "feminine" as it sometimes evokes an emotional response as the word sounds similar to "feminism." According to Wikipedia, feminism is defined as a range of movements and ideologies that share a common goal: to define, establish, and achieve equal political, economic, cultural, personal, and social rights for women. My request is that you refrain from linking these two very different words to each other, and think about the word feminine in a solely descriptive sense, as in a quality of softness and vulnerability, an opening toward something new.

The Feminine Advantage

When women embody the strengths in the FLM, they drop into something that is much stronger than using force, aggression, or command & control, as traditional approaches have dictated in the past. When women give themselves permission to fully embody these strengths, they drop into an ancient power, connected to the earth, to something bigger than just themselves. This power lives in the body, and our intuition is the access point to our strength and wisdom. When women learn how to heal the wounds they've carried for far too long and learn how to channel their feminine energy, they can tap into a power that is beyond anything they ever imagined. Therefore, many of the exercises you'll find in this book are designed to help you tap into the wisdom of your body through building trust, integrity and self-acceptance with yourself.

The beauty of tapping into our true power is that when we do, the need to control or to compete dissipates. We don't need to be "ice queens" or "bitches" anymore! We don't have to struggle and take the burden of the world on our shoulders just to prove our worth and value! We don't even need to compromise who we are or hide our opinions! There is true freedom in embodying our true feminine power, and with that freedom comes ease, grace, and pure joy. Instead of living with the depletion, burnout, and stress that accumulates over time, we can begin to thrive by embracing who we are at our core.

So why should we take the risk of embodying the feminine in our leadership approach? Speaking from my personal experience, here is what I know to be possible. When we are allowed to be authentic, bringing *all* parts of ourselves to the table, it can build our confidence, because we no longer have to censor or second-guess ourselves. Flexing our intuitive and perceptive minds, we can build integrity by learning to trust the decisions we make. Getting out of our own way and asking for help and softening into our vulnerability can make us more accessible to others, more human, more approachable. People will be compelled to follow because they sense confidence in us. By listening and trusting more, we can become inclusive leaders where the people who work for them or with them feel heard, acknowledged, and part of a larger purpose. This all leads to more fulfillment, satisfaction, and motivation, leading to better performance, creativity, and innovation on our teams.

It's a domino effect that can have a lasting and positive impact on the people you work with, the teams you manage, and the customers you serve.

Did I mention the added benefit? When you are able to reclaim your power and lead from your authentic self, as if by magic, men will feel invited to collaborate as true and equal partners. Instead of being intimidated by women's overt faux-masculine strength, men will feel invited to contribute, collaborate and work alongside women. They'll feel safer to show more vulnerability, maybe even feel safer to show their softer, more emotional sides. This will strengthen your relationship with other men, and allow for a flowering of a beautiful partnership where both parties can give of their best, leaning into each other's strengths and being able to work together from a foundation of trust and support.

The possibilities of improving your relationship with men are limitless, and it can transform not only your professional working relationships, but also your romantic relationships as well. (That's for another book, but I can definitely assure you— your romantic life will never be the same!). Also, you'll notice that your relationships with women will shift. The tendency to be competitive or judgmental will fade away. Feeling intimidated or jealous of other women's abilities or achievements won't be a thing anymore. You'll find yourself wanting to support women to thrive, and you'll realize the importance of encouraging each other's success. And in this day and age where women face so many obstacles, forming supportive communities of women is an integral piece for women's advancement in all areas and in all parts of the globe.

Because we are still dealing with the traditional notion that leadership and success are associated with more masculine traits, not only do we have to redefine leadership for ourselves so that we can shatter these stereotypes, we have to find a way to navigate the landscape that still exists currently. In Chapter 2, we'll look at how to create the foundation necessary to evolve and transcend the current paradigm that exists by first looking at the relationship we have with ourselves. This requires self-awareness, understanding, and a level of skill that luckily women are biologically hard-wired for. This is according to new neuroscience data that I'll be introducing in Chapter 3, where we look at the differences between masculine and feminine leadership strengths.

In Chapters 4-10, I'll dive deeper into each of the 7 Feminine Strengths & 4 Masculine Traits of the Feminine Leadership Model™ offering specific exercises that will help you develop these strengths and traits, as well as offer tips, resources and stories from other female executives and entrepreneurs who successfully embody the Feminine Leadership style. In Chapter 11, I'll talk about how to create movements that bring about change, and how you can keep the conversation going.

This book is intended as a self-coaching guide to help you develop the capacity to lead using a new approach. Whether you lead a team of people in an organization, are a budding manager, or run a business or non-profit, you can take the concepts presented in this book and put them into action immediately through the exercises presented. To that end, I invite you to delve into this book with an open mind and open heart. The exercises are designed as a tool to help you reflect, create self-awareness, and lead you to mastery. I ask that you take the time to do the exercises highlighted in each chapter, as it will deepen your experience of the concepts presented. For some, the exercises might be a bit touchy-feely and for others, they won't be a big deal. Many of the exercises ask you to journal about your findings and about your reflections. While not a requirement, I find that it helps my clients in their learning and development, so I encourage you to do the same.

Self-reflection can sometimes be challenging, especially if you are attempting it alone without the assistance of a coach or mentor, but it is a critical step to becoming a conscious leader, and it activates feminine qualities of leadership. I encourage you to find a buddy or a group of women with whom you can read the book and support one another as you go through it. Let's build a community of like-minded women instead of creating change in isolation, as is usually the case in the current masculine paradigm. Only through creating a critical mass will we be able to make the changes necessary to turn the tide and create more equilibrium in ourselves and in our world.

CHAPTER 2
Redefining the Relationship With Ourselves

How Do You Relate to Your Femininity?

Before moving further, it would be helpful for you to explore your own relationship with the meaning of the word "feminine." Many people have different reactions to this word, but women who might have shut down this part of themselves could carry around some wounding about how they relate to their femininity. Wherever you are in your journey, it would be helpful for you to reflect and define it for yourself before moving forward. The following exercises will help you gain more clarity about how you can incorporate the qualities of the feminine in your life and leadership style.

Exercise #1

1. Think about all the things you associate with being a woman and write them down.

2. Then, write down a list of all the things you associate with the word feminine.

3. Compare your lists and reflect on the similarities and differences.

Questions for Reflection

1. Reflect on your lists. What words did you choose? What does that tell you about your view of womanhood and the feminine?

2. In what way are your lists similar or different?

3. Do you feel you relate more to one list or the other? What situations or experiences have led you to that?

4. Are there any aspects from either list that you would like more of? Less of? What would that give you?

5. How can you incorporate those qualities you want more of into your life and leadership style?

Healing Our Wounding

The objectification of women and the current sensationalist media landscape have severely affected our ability to own our true power. The way we view ourselves has changed because of it, and it's also sadly impacted the way men treat women. All of this has led to developing sometimes unhealthy relationships with our bodies, sexuality and power. The relationship we have with our sexuality has a direct link to how we carry our power, as those two things are interconnected. The best way to explore this is through the Eastern philosophy of 'chakras' or power centers located in the body.

If you've ever done yoga or meditation, you might be familiar with the second chakra or the sacral chakra as it is also called, located two inches below the navel and rooted into the spine. This power center holds our basic needs for sexuality, creativity, intuition, and self-worth. It is also about friendliness, creativity, and emotions. It governs sense of self-worth, confidence in our creativity, and the ability to relate to others in an open and friendly way. Proper balance in this chakra means the ability to flow with emotions freely and to feel and reach out to others sexually. If this chakra is blocked, a person may feel emotionally explosive, manipulative, obsessed with thoughts of sex or may lack energy.

In other words, the second chakra is the creative life force center and also happens to be where actual life is created and birthed. This is also where our true expression lives, and from where our gifts and talents originate. Many women who give birth report a feeling of real power when igniting this chakra during childbirth. But for the rest of the time, this area of our bodies lays dormant, and unfortunately becomes a source of shame for many women as they develop negative relationships with their bodies and their sexuality. Interestingly, many women carry unwanted weight in this area, perhaps as a means of protection. My belief is that over time, we have become disconnected from this chakra, the source of our true power, due to objectification and victimization of women, which can affect how we view ourselves, our self-confidence, and how we express our feminine nature as well.

Healing the shame and wounding and connecting into our source of power are important steps in moving from victimhood to empowerment. When we give ourselves the chance to explore the hurt and pain passed down from generations and perpetuated by the media (bullying, sexism, or abusive treatment), we can take back our power and our feminine strength. It is the first step in moving towards more balance and in reclaiming our voice, our creativity, confidence, and our effectiveness as leaders.

Exercise #2

This following exercise is to clear away any negative thoughts or associations you might be carrying about your womanhood or femininity.

1. Take a moment to reflect on any feelings of shame, woundedness, victimhood, or pain that you associate with being a woman or your femininity.

2. Write down all the words that come to mind as you reflect on this. Make a list of all the negative thoughts or associations you carry. Try not to think 'too hard'; let them flow naturally.

3. Once you are finished, create a ritual to cleanse yourself of those feelings: you might want to burn

the piece of paper, throw it into the sea, flush it down the drain, whatever works for you.

4. Now spend some time thinking of all the positive qualities you would like to embody and carry around with you as they relate to your womanhood and femininity. Give yourself time to reflect and to journal about how you can more fully express and access your feminine nature. Create structures and accountability that will help you achieve this.

Fire in the Belly

Although I didn't realize it, there was a time when I also shut down this part of myself. I carried a lot of shame from being bullied and teased as a child, where I learned that being me was not OK. As I became a young adult and attended an all-girls Catholic high school, I was even more confused about who I was, and I began to lose my voice, my true expression, and was taught to shun my sexuality. Over time I learned to play small, kept my head down, was a good student, and generally did as I was told. I was the proverbial "good girl." As I did that, I unknowingly gave away my power, which extended well into my 20s and led me to make some decisions that weren't very empowered.

Thankfully, there was a turning point that helped me regain my sense of power. It happened during a year-long leadership program, where one of our challenges was to do a ropes course, which included climbing a 40 foot tree. My task was to climb the tree, get all the way to the top, walk down a wooden plank and then jump out of the tree. The only safety net I had was a helmet and a harness. As I looked up at that tree, I could feel my fight-or-flight response in full force, and all I wanted to do was run away as fast as possible. There was NO way I was getting up that tree! My mind was telling me "I can't, I really can't" as I watched women twice my age, in half my shape, climb the tree no problem.

I was really familiar with the words "I can't"—those two words had played over and over again in my head all my life. They had prevented me from trying new things, reaching for my dreams, voicing my opinion, and taking risks. I was very familiar with those two words, and deep down inside I knew that I only had one choice if I wanted to ever overcome the power those menacing words held over me. I had to climb that damn tree!

So I got up on the ladder and then proceeded to put one foot on a tiny metal rung on the side of the tree, my heart racing, palms sweating, not daring to look down. I was so scared!! All I could hear were my teammates rooting me on, encouraging me, supporting me from below, which gave me the courage to keep going. Suddenly as I found myself clinging to the side of that beautiful redwood tree for dear life, something profound happened. My mind went blank. All the negative thoughts went away. Actually, there were no more thoughts at all, and all my awareness dropped into my body, specifically into my belly, the second chakra. I felt this amazing energy, this fire coming from my belly, and I instinctively knew that if I trusted my body, I would be able to climb the rest of that tree. So I did, and like a Jedi master, made it to the top in no time. As I stood gazing down 40-feet, I knew I had tapped into something truly powerful, something that would change my life forever.

After some reflection, what I realized I had tapped into was my creative life force, my true power. If this energy could get ME up a 40-foot tree, then you bet it was powerful! It could move mountains! This is the single most powerful energy women have available to them, but besides childbirth and a few moments here or there, we are absolutely not leveraging it in the slightest. It's where our intuition comes from, as well as our ability to be centered and grounded, which are essential components of the FLM. I continued tapping into this power center to allow my intuition to become stronger, unleashing my creativity, which I channeled into my leadership approach, in both life and in business.

The results for me have been powerful. By cultivating this inner power I began to feel more confident, I was able to make decisions more quickly, take bigger risks, and most important-ly, I was more easily able to follow my heart. This eventually led me to leave my career in marketing and pursue my pas-sion in helping people through executive coaching and train-ing. I launched Highest Path Consulting, went on to launch the Women & Power Leadership Forum, as well as the Wom-en Making a Difference podcast, and became a writer for the Huffington Post about women's leadership topics. By follow-ing my heart, I've lived in places like Italy, New York City, and Los Angeles, but most importantly, I'm able to make a positive impact in the world through my work.

But here's the thing—unfortunately, this power has been shut down in many women through millennia. However, if we can learn to tap into it and start embracing it as a strength, I truly believe it has the power and potential to effect change. It can also aid in manifesting everything we want, from the per-fect relationship to impactful social and political movements, to effectively leading teams toward more innovation. The best way to do that is through healing the wounding and pain that women hold in this area of our bodies, and to develop a healthy relationship with our innate creativity by activating our core power.

Energizing Your Core Power

Exercise #3

To help you harness your core power, I invite you to do the following visualization exercise:

Wherever you are, get comfortable and take a few deep breaths. Now imagine dropping your energy down into your root chakra, the first chakra. Imagine a long cord going down from your root, anchoring you into the center of the earth. With the following breath, allow all of the tension to move out of your body.

Next, drop your attention into your second chakra. Breathe into this area, which lies 2 inches below your navel, and 2 inches in from there. Begin activating this area, by imagining heat building up or imagining a white ball of light igniting in this area. Feel that sensation for a few minutes. Notice what happens. Allow this part of your body to become engaged and activated. If there are any places that feel numb or stuck, shine more light onto it. Do this until you feel that whole area activated.

Next, stand up, and with your feet planted securely into the floor, with your hands on the second chakra, feel the energy moving up, into your belly. Up from your belly, into your solar plexus, up into your heart, into your throat, then to your forehead and into the top of your head. Pull that energy upward and expand it outward toward all corners of the room.

Once you are ready, open your eyes and just notice what has shifted. Journal your answers to the following questions:

1. Was it easy or hard to access your second chakra?

2. Did you feel something get unstuck in that area?

3. Did you feel more energized or more alive after doing the visualization?

4. Did anything wake up in you—a desire to create, express or something that wanted to come forth?

   2nd Chakra exercise

5. What else did you notice?

As the day goes on, observe what happens and how this exercise made an impact on your day. Practice this at least once a day for two weeks, and consider making it part of your daily routine to help you stay engaged with your creativity and power. This exercise might be difficult for you or could bring up strong emotions, including grief or anger. Breathe into those feelings, and stay with the exercise. The more we can process those emotions, become aware of them, accept them and give them a voice, the more easily we can let them go and shift out of them. You might also try working with a coach or trusted friend if it becomes too difficult or challenging.

Women have other strengths that they aren't leveraging as much as they could, and I am going to address those in the rest of this book. But since tapping into our core power is so fundamental, I wanted to dedicate a special chapter to it because I believe it is the first step to embracing our true feminine power and leadership. Once you have accomplished this, the rest becomes much easier, and will support you in the journey toward embodying Feminine Leadership and transforming your life, your relationships, and your impact in the world.

CHAPTER 3
Masculine vs. Feminine Leadership Styles

Transformational vs. Transactional Leadership

According to a recent study featured in the Harvard Business Review's *Women and the Labyrinth of Leadership*, meta-analysis was done integrating the results of 45 studies addressing the question of what might be a distinctive female leadership style. To compare leadership skills, the researchers adopted a framework introduced by leadership scholar James MacGregor Burns that distinguishes between transformational leadership and transactional leadership.

Transformational leaders establish themselves as role models by gaining followers' trust and confidence. They state future goals, develop plans to achieve those goals, and innovate, even when their organizations are generally successful. Such leaders mentor and empower followers, encouraging them to develop their full potential so they can contribute more effectively to their organizations.

By contrast, transactional leaders establish give-and-take relationships that appeal to subordinates self-interest. Such leaders manage in the conventional manner of clarifying employee responsibilities, rewarding them for meeting objectives, and correcting them for failing to meet objectives. The meta-analysis found that in general, female leaders were somewhat more transformational than male leaders, especially when it came to giving support and encouragement to employees. They also engaged in more of the rewarding behaviors that are one aspect of transactional leadership.

Meanwhile, men exceeded women on the aspects of transactional leadership involving corrective and disciplinary actions that are either active (timely) or passive (belated). Men were also more likely than women to be laissez-faire leaders, who take little responsibility for managing. The research tells us not only that men and women do have somewhat different leadership styles, but also that women's approaches are the more generally effective—while men's often are only somewhat effective or actually hinder effectiveness. So why then is it that many women struggle with embodying this style, and feel compelled to emulate a more transactional style of leadership that is more common in men? To understand that, we have to look at the history of leadership and what it means to have power.

Control vs. Power

For eons people have been controlled by the need to dominate and control others as a means to be "powerful." If we look at the current state of affairs of the world, many of the problems we see can be traced back to the need for power and control. Who will control the world's oil reserves? Which party has control of Congress? How will we control our borders? The list goes on and on. We have been, and still are, motivated by our need for control as a human species.

The traditional meaning of power can be described with masculine words like dominating, control, aggressive, authoritarian, and so on. Interestingly, those are also words that have traditionally been associated with leadership. And in fact, if we look at the last century, we can see many examples of world leaders who embodied these qualities. As we came into the Industrial Age in the 20th century, this type of command and control leadership style was adopted since it was best suited for maximizing output in factories and growing infrastructure. As women came into the workplace, they adopted these notions of power and leadership style that were already in place. In my opinion, not only is this counter to our nature as women, it also is an outdated model that no longer applies to the modern workplace. As we move from the Industrial Age to the Information Age, output is no longer solely measured in units made. Instead, it is now measured in new ideas, solutions, and technology, which require innovation, creativity, and collaboration.

In order to stimulate and inspire people toward creating and innovating, we must begin to redefine our meaning of power. The 21st century is requiring us to completely rethink our notions of power, dominance, and aggression. By facing some of the biggest challenges that humanity has ever faced, we are being required to move from command and control to collaboration and community. Organizations realize that to stay competitive they need to develop cultures where everyone can do their best work, not only to thrive but to stimulate innovation that will keep them ahead of the curve. The command and control approach that was needed in the 20th century no longer serves our collective aspirations.

One of the best examples of companies that value collaboration is, you guessed it, Google. With over 30,000 employees, the company has been voted #1 on Fortune's list of 100 Best Companies to Work For, not just one, but five times. So what's so great about Google, besides the free meals and snacks they provide their employees? What Google understands inherently is that innovation and great ideas come from people working together in a collaborative way. So they do this by creating opportunities for collaboration. For instance, their flexible workspace is designed in such a way as to encourage ideas to emerge between peers through spontaneous chats. At one point, all employees were allowed to devote 20% of their time to new ideas and special projects, giving way to two of their biggest products, Gmail and AdSense. By giving their employees time and space to create and innovate, Google has built one of the largest and most profitable companies in the world. And we see that more and more companies, especially in the tech space, are adopting ways for people to collaborate because they know it drives innovation in the new economy we're operating in.

And yet many organizations, as well as governments and institutions are still struggling with this reversal in power structure. But what we are seeing are individuals waking up to their individual power and using that power to make positive change through collaboration. We see that now with the power of social media, in the current tech-boom and the emerging sharing economy with companies like AirBnb, Lynda.com, and Uber developing platforms to share resources, knowledge, and skills. We are seeing it in politics globally, with people uprisings like the Arab Spring. We see it with the Black Lives Matter movement, which is about fighting ongoing racism in America. We even saw it in grassroots movements like Occupy Wall Street, which fought against growing inequality. We are collectively reshaping the meaning of the word "power" as we speak, and it's a wildly exciting time to be alive and witness where this takes us.

The same thing is happening for women, not only in the West but globally. For example, just recently women in Saudi Arabia won the chance to vote and hold political office. In India, they are finally putting laws into place to protect women from rape and violence. And in the US, women are waking up to the fact that they are still under-represented and under-paid in the workforce. We see a third wave of feminism emerging, with women demanding more equality, and fighting to defend rights that we have fought so hard to obtain, including a woman's right to choose. All of these examples have emerged because of the grass-roots efforts led by millions of women and men who have mobilized and worked together toward a common goal.

The exciting thing is that as women begin to wake up and reclaim their power, they are realizing that their true power lies not in their ability to control others, but in their ability to inspire others. A great example of this is Malala Yousafzai, who was recently awarded the Nobel Peace prize. After a horrendous attack at her school by the Taliban in Pakistan, where she was shot in the head and survived, Malala's message is about forgiveness and peace instead of retribution. As more women lean into their gifts and capacities, they offer a new approach to tackling our big challenges. As women heal their wounding, they realize true power lies in their ability to forgive and to practice empathy and compassion. By doing so, we will become trailblazers in how human beings relate to one another. And that is the real change the world needs right now as we shift into a society that values feminine qualities of connection, interdependence, community, and collaboration.

Men and Women's Brains

What is also exciting is recent neuroscience research supporting the idea that women have gifts and abilities that are unique to them. As much as we want to believe that there is nothing different between us and our male counterparts, there is new research that begs to differ. In a study by the University of Pennsylvania, after studying the brains of 1000 men and women, they discovered a major difference in the wiring of their brains. In male brains they found greater neural connectivity from front to back and within one hemisphere, while in females, between the left and right hemispheres. This results in a big difference in how men and women behave. The study, authored by Ragini Verma, associate professor in Penn's Perelman School of Medicine's department of Radiology, featured in the *Proceedings of the National Academy of Sciences (PNAS)*, is one of the largest to compare the "connectomes"—comprehensive maps of neural connections in the brains—of male and female humans.

For their study, Prof. Verma and her colleagues used a highly sensitive form of MRI (Magnetic Resonance Imaging) known as diffusion sensor imaging which tracks water travelling along nerve fibers. Highlighting these water tracks produces a detailed map of the pathways connecting different regions of the brain. What they discovered was that women seem to be anatomically wired towards intuitive thinking and collaborative decision making, and are better listeners and can multi-task better than men. Men are wired towards perceptive and sensorimotor skills, like throwing a ball and playing sports, as well as single tasks.

When asked about the findings, Prof. Verma said that the greatest surprise was how much the findings supported old stereotypes, with men's brains apparently wired more for perception and coordinated actions, and women's for social skills and memory, making them better equipped for multitasking. "If you look at functional studies, the left of the brain is more for logical thinking, the right of the brain is for more intuitive thinking. So if there's a task that involves doing both of those things, it would seem that women are hard-wired to do those better," Verma said. "Women are better at intuitive thinking. Women are better at remembering things. When you talk, women are more emotionally involved—they will listen more." Verma goes on to say that "these maps show us a stark difference—and complementarity—in the architecture of the human brain that helps provide a potential neural basis as to why men excel at certain tasks, and women at others." Co-author Ruben C. Gur, professor of psychology in Penn's department of Psychiatry, says: "It's quite striking how complementary the brains of women and men really are." Previous studies have shown brain differences between the sexes, but not to the extent of highlighting differences in neural wiring, and not in such a large population, say the researchers.

Of course, this research is in its early days, and experts have questioned whether it can be that simple, arguing it is a huge leap to extrapolate from anatomical differences to try to explain behavioral variation between the sexes. Also, brain connections are not set and can change throughout life. So it's very possible that women can develop or learn skills dominant in men or vice versa. But when we look at what we are naturally born with and predisposed to, this data does suggest that there are some differences. The piece that's important for women to realize is that these skills seem to be an integral part of our make-up. And there is nothing wrong with owning that fact and leveraging our gifts, and learning to work well with the opposite sex to achieve greater results.

The good news is that neuroscience is proving that behavior is learned, not just inherited. For a long time, scientists believed behavior was set in stone and it couldn't really be changed. But through recent studies, we are seeing that people can in fact pave new neural pathways leading to new behaviors. This is promising because whether you are a man, woman or transgender, whatever "gifts" you may or may not have, and wherever you fall on the spectrum, you do indeed have the power to learn new traits and behaviors that can help you be a better leader.

The not so good news is that for far too long, women in business have worked hard to hide their strengths, fearing it would hurt them in the long run. We have learned to judge ourselves, giving into gender biases that say "care" and "nurture" are a weakness. As a result, we've grown to be more logical than intuitive, we've been quick to judge rather than listen and practice empathy, and we've led people by command and control rather than by collaborative decision making. I believe this has had a damaging impact on women's leadership ability, how they are perceived, how they feel on a day-to day-basis, and has ultimately contributed to the gender gap that exists in organizations today. The time has come to bring back some of the qualities that people are looking for in their leaders, rather than try so hard to fit in and lead like men.

The Athena Doctrine

According to a global survey of 64,000 responders, 66% believed that the world would be a better place if men thought more like women, as featured in *The Athena Doctrine* by John Gerzema & Michael D'Antonio. Those respondents were then asked to classify and rate masculine and feminine leadership traits, and to rate which of those qualities they preferred in their leaders. It was shown that people far preferred leaders that exhibited feminine traits, which they identified as patience, loyalty, empathy, and long-term thinking, rather than masculine traits such as dominance and aggression. Clearly this shows a shift happening around the world toward a collective yearning for a different style of leadership to emerge.

The importance of *The Athena Doctrine* study, according to their analysis, was a shift toward leaders that were more "expressive, sharing feelings and emotions more openly and honestly," which shows us that authenticity in leaders is something that people want more of. The days of the stoic, unemotional leader are long gone. Watch out, hedge fund managers—the results also show that people want long-term thinkers who can think beyond short-term gains for stakeholders, to strategically create a sustainable future for both the business and outside stakeholders (such as the community or the planet). As we move toward a more interconnected world and we realize the impact that our decisions can make on literally the entire globe, people are looking for leaders to be more inclusive. Instead of a top-down, more masculine approach, people want an atmosphere of collaboration and consensus in decision-making. And it's a good thing too, because this is exactly what leads to innovation in the 21st century.

The Athena study also showed that people valued masculine qualities such as being decisive and resilient. Women sometimes struggle with these two qualities, mainly because of our lack of self-confidence. When we waver in our decisions, we can be perceived as being indecisive which sometimes stems from self-doubt. Being able to trust your gut and lean into your intuition can help with this and we'll be examining how to do that later in the book. Also, bouncing back from failures and being able to take risks are fundamental to good leadership, which is why building resilience is so important for women, and one of the traits of the FLM.

What this tells us is there is a time and a place to bring in masculine qualities. We need both to be effective. Like when we need to get our point across more clearly, to make quick decisions under stress, or to bounce back from a perceived failure or mistake. In fact, these are important qualities for any leader in order to maximize effectiveness. And that is why the FLM features four distinct masculine qualities women can leverage, and I will be addressing how to use these for maximum effectiveness in combination with feminine strengths. When we are balanced, we have access to a broad range of capacities that can improve the way we build relationships, how we communicate and how we lead others. The key is to have situational awareness and to be able to determine in the moment which qualities we can use to most easily and gracefully reach our desired impact.

Creating the Balance

We are now at the forefront of this shift toward more inclusion, interdependence and collaboration in business and beyond, and it affects both men and women. To find better balance in leadership by incorporating both masculine *and* feminine traits requires an exploration and expression of the feminine to balance out the highly masculine and disempowered feminine state we've been in for some time, not only in the corporate world but more broadly. Once we are able to create this shift in ourselves, it will then be reflected outwardly, to create harmony and more equilibrium around us. Anything that is in the extreme eventually loses effectiveness, and so what is important to remember is that as leaders, we need to be adaptable and be able to pick and choose which qualities are necessary in any given situation. Leading with a very masculine or very feminine approach can have less than desirable results. So again, the aim is balance and integration as we walk the tightrope of leadership.

The 4 Quadrants of Leadership

To take this to a practical level, let's look at how women are perceived in the workplace. It's easy to know what it means to be "powerful" in the traditional sense of the word, but what does it look like when we are powerfully standing in the Feminine? Many of us have different associations with the word "feminine," most of which do not equate with leadership or power. Think back to the exercise you did in Chapter 2, where I asked you make a list of words you associate with the word 'feminine.' You might have come up with words like softness, vulnerability, intuition, and receptivity, among others. Not surprisingly, most of us don't associate that with leadership or power. And most of us probably don't bring those qualities into the workplace in large doses. How often are you willing to be vulnerable in front of your co-workers or peers and ask for help? How willing are you to let go of control, stop micro-managing, and trust others? Do you believe you'll be perceived as weak, incompetent, undeserving, or unvalued if you express any of those qualities?

The truth is that there are some distinctions when we talk about the masculine and feminine. To clarify, I want to present the 4 Quadrants of Leadership: Empowered Feminine, Empowered Masculine, Disempowered Feminine and Disempowered Masculine.

4 QUADRANTS OF LEADERSHIP

EMPOWERED FEMININE	EMPOWERED MASCULINE
Centered	Direct
Visionary	Resilient
Vulnerable	Assertive
Caring	Daring
Empathic	Confident
Intuitive	Curious
Collaborative	Flexible
Humble	Strategic
Grounded	Emotional Intelligence
Multiple-Stakeholder focused	Multiple-Stakeholder focused
DISEMPOWERED MASCULINE	**DISEMPOWERED FEMININE**
Dominating	Powerless
Command/Control	Victimized
Aggressive	Blameful
Fear-based	Angry
Manipulative	Withdrawn
Hierarchical	Over-analytical
Insecure	Competitive
Ego driven	Self-doubt
Scarcity based	Manipulative
Short-term thinking	Dramatic

Let's start with the Empowered Feminine and Empowered Masculine. When we as women are standing fully in the upper two quadrants, we are grounded and centered, fully aligned with our head, heart, and gut. We are able to inspire others with our strong vision and compelling message, being assertive without alienating others. We are able to ask for help and allow others to fully contribute. We are able to drop into our intuition and trust it for guidance in decision-making, helping us be decisive but also willing to take risks when necessary. We are able to use our emotions as a vehicle to understand ourselves and others. We are resilient, easily bouncing back from failure. We are able to motivate and engage those we lead with a collaborative approach, while leaving our ego at the door and giving credit where credit is due. This is the impact women leaders can have when they are balanced and integrating qualities on the spectrum between the Empowered Masculine and Feminine.

However, the truth is that sometimes we believe that if we do express these traits, we will lose our credibility, authority, and power in the workplace. We are afraid to be mocked by our peers, or that people will take advantage, or perceive us as incapable, not intelligent, indecisive, or weak. The antidote many have chosen thus far has been to overcompensate by putting up a tough exterior, control as much as possible, take on as much as possible, and be as logical and unemotional as possible. This ends up pulling us away from our center, from the very essence of what makes us who we are as women. It leads us away from the feminine and into a 'faux-masculine' place that is neither authentic nor effective for most.

When we are in this Disempowered Masculine state, there is a doubly negative impact for women's integrity, likeability and authenticity. As a result, you might notice a lack of motivation, inspiration, or engagement on the teams you lead. You might notice your employees are just unable to think outside the box or come to you with any creative solutions. What you may not know is that people secretly don't like working with you and are too afraid to tell you to your face. You might be taking on too much workload instead of delegating, which limits your ability to reach toward career advancement and can negatively affect work/life balance. Worst of all, you might be stifling creativity and innovation critical to the success of your team and your organization. This creates obstacles to your confidence as well as to your ability to move upward, and this is where most women get frustrated, overwhelmed, or burned out, and end up opting out instead of leaning in.

On the other hand, some women can be in the Disempowered Feminine, where they hide their opinions, don't speak up, act too humble, keep their head down and hope someone will notice one day how competent they are in hopes of earning a promotion. They hide behind the shadows, not expressing their true feelings or ideas, and end up feeling resentful, not included or victimized. From a leadership perspective, this can be detrimental to our effectiveness as leaders. Needless to say it will be difficult to have authority, you may not aim for challenges outside your comfort zone, you'll probably not lead your team well if you're in a management position, and it will be difficult to have influence or visibility across the organization. Of course these are extreme examples and there can be many shades of grey, but it's important to make this distinction because of the very different impacts of each quadrant. When we are fully standing in our Empowered Feminine and balancing it out with Empowered Masculine traits, we can be strong, confident, decisive, and firm without being a "bulldog" or a "bitch." The negative associations of the word "feminine" go out the window. All you have left is a woman who can get the job done in a way that doesn't alienate people and opens the door for collaboration and inclusiveness.

The First Step: Awareness

Exercise #4

The first step in any sort of behavior change is awareness. Finding the balance in our leadership style is integral if women are to be effective and liked by their peers. For women (and men) to be better leaders they must first become aware of where they currently fall on the leadership spectrum. Once we become aware of our impact and understand how we are perceived, we can be free to make choices and decide whether it makes sense to adopt a different approach.

Take a moment to reflect on the diagram above of the 4 Quadrants of Leadership. Make a list of words that best describes your current leadership style. Looking at your list, do you fall in any one quadrant or a combination of quadrants? Which is more dominant for you? Reflect on the impact of your current leadership style and journal about your findings.

Balancing the Feminine and Masculine

Achieving balance between the Empowered Feminine and Masculine is what we're aiming for. For some, you may be in one of those quadrants more often, so looking at the opposing quadrant will help you find that balance. For others, you might be in either side of the lower quadrants, so your challenge and areas of development will be to achieve more empowered states. For example, if you tend to be directive and like to micro-manage, working on collaboration could help you achieve more trust and in turn more engagement with your peers or employees. Or if you are dominating, you might need to practice vulnerability in order to step back and let others have a voice or contribute. Or you might be withdrawn, feel like a victim or powerless, so working on your confidence might help you be more self-assured. In general, being either too masculine or too feminine usually keeps us from having the desired impact we want to have. When we stay in one extreme or the other for too long, we become imbalanced and fall out of harmony with ourselves and others.

Another example is the double bind women get stuck in when trying to assert themselves. Studies have shown that if women are overly directive or authoritative, it can come off as being "bitchy," while men are perceived as leaders. Going to the other extreme like being vague and beating around the bush obviously isn't going to work either. Because stereotypes around how men and women should behave are still mostly ingrained, women have more of a challenge in finding the right balance and approach when asserting themselves. There is a happy medium, where we can voice our opinions with strength, coming from our core when we are totally centered and present. From this place, women can sound just as convincing and authoritative as the next guy, without the nasty label.

The next part of this exercise is to reflect on which quadrants will help you balance out your leadership style. Look at the qualities in that quadrant, write them down and put them somewhere prominent (I personally like sticky notes on my computer screen or mirror at home). Think of situations in the recent past where you could have used these qualities. What would the impact have been? What would you have done differently? Look for situations in your workplace where you can incorporate these qualities, perhaps at an upcoming meeting with an employee, or a conversation with your boss. Commit to practicing this when the situation arises, and then notice the impact of what happens when you do.

The Likeability Gap

In a recent Gallop poll survey, women responded that they preferred to work with a male boss rather than a female boss. Not only is this a sad state of affairs, but it also describes the unintended consequences when women adopt a more masculine style of leadership. We all remember the Meryl Streep character in *The Devil Wears Prada*. Obviously that was an exaggeration of your typical Queen Bee, a female executive who is dominating, cold, controlling and outright mean. There are many shades of grey here, but many of us have experienced working with a woman (or a man) who was overly intimidating, controlling, or competitive. Some of us have quit jobs, or even worse, endured the sheer torture of working for someone like her. As much as we want to think this only happens in the movies, the reality is that the Queen Bee syndrome is still very much alive and rampant, and can be an obstacle in women's advancement in the workplace.

As much as we want to blame men, gender politics, or sexism for the lack of women in leadership positions, I think it's only fair to first point the finger at ourselves. Women must take into account that one of the reasons they are not advancing as quickly as they would like might have to do with the likeability factor. Obviously no one wants to work with someone they don't like. And if women are showing up in ways that make them difficult to work with (e.g., a Queen Bee), then chances are they are going to be passed up for promotions and advancement. And even if they do move up the ladder, their lack of people skills and emotional intelligence will keep them from producing the results expected of them. Or at the very least, no one will enjoy working with them, which again leads to poor results.

Annie Hyman Pratt talks about her experience when she took over her family's business, Coffee Bean & Tea Leaf. She jumped in feet first, not ever having the experience of managing teams or running a company. At the beginning she decided her approach, given her Type-A personality, was to get involved in all the details surrounding the business. She prided herself on being a micro-manager, very detail-oriented and having tight control over all departments. But soon, she began hearing rumors that some of her employees thought of her as an "ice queen," and they thought she wasn't very approachable and even seemed to be slightly intimidated by her.

Learning how her staff negatively perceived her was a huge wake up-call for Annie, and after some reflection, she decided to change her approach as a leader. Instead of micro-managing, she let go of control but at the same time empowered her teams to take ownership of specific projects, and gave them more authority to make decisions. She consciously chose vulnerability as the pathway to build relationships and partnerships. Her motto became "Learn what you're good at, and then ask for help where you need it." Her meetings turned into discussions that led to experimentation, inspiring her teams to try something new and iterate from there, instead of having to be directive and telling people what to do. Ideas started flowing and for maybe the first time in her role as CEO, she found herself listening to what people had to say. This led to one of the biggest innovations at Coffee Bean.

"For a long time, we had been getting feedback from customers that they didn't feel the customer experience was very warm and friendly like one would expect at their local coffee shop. Drinks were getting mixed up, and the overall experience wasn't well executed. We were having a discussion about this internally one day, and someone had the idea of taking people's names with their drink orders. In the past I might have just brushed the idea aside, and although I was a little skeptical, I chose to be more open to employee's ideas. So we decided to pilot this idea in one of our stores and it was a total success. People loved the personal touch, it made the drink order line flow more fluidly, and it positively impacted the customer experience. Eventually we rolled this out to all of our stores, and it became so popular that later on, one of our biggest competitors stole the idea!"

The type of leadership Annie exhibited is what I call Feminine Leadership. Leaning into the feminine qualities of being able to listen, staying open to new ideas, incorporating input and feedback, and also learning to ask for help, led her company to one of the biggest innovations in the coffee industry. It goes to show that Feminine Leadership doesn't just make sense, it makes economic and business sense as well. All of this sounds well and good, but getting to where Annie got doesn't always come easy. It usually takes a coming to Jesus or a total meltdown, neither of which is much fun. The other less painful way is to create self-awareness, as well as to develop and cultivate a more inclusive and balanced approach to leadership, designed for women.

Impact of Your Leadership Style

Exercise #5

The quiz below will help you gauge the impact of your leadership approach to determine how inclusive you are as a leader. Take a moment to reflect on each question and then use the rating scale to rate each answer accordingly:

- Never (-2)
- I'd like to (0)
- Definitely (2)
- Unsure (-1)
- Sometimes (1)

1. I tend to identify with Empowered Feminine traits as it relates to my personal leadership approach, including intuition, empathy, and vulnerability. _____

2. When managing others, I tend to use a coach approach vs. a directive approach to help develop the necessary skill set for the task at hand. _____

3. I like to build relationships with others in the workplace, and do this on a consistent basis. _____

4. I listen actively and deeply when others speak. _____

5. I ask my team for input and feedback and I brainstorm ideas with them on a consistent basis. _____

6. I am able to admit when I am wrong or when I don't have the answer, and I ask for help. _____

7. I like to look at the long-term picture and think strategically about the impact of my decisions. _____

8. I tend to often give others the benefit of the doubt or try to see things from their perspective. _____

9. I am able to easily delegate tasks, trust my team, and empower them to get the job done. _____

10. I make sure to take the time to give credit to those on my team when they deserve it and acknowledge their efforts. _____

Tally up your answers. The most you can score on this quiz is 20, which means you are exhibiting and embodying a balanced and inclusive leadership style. This exercise is meant to function as a compass and, depending on your score, bring you some added awareness about the impact of your personal leadership style.

In the upcoming chapters, I'll be suggesting ways in which you can achieve a more balanced and inclusive leadership approach. No matter what your beliefs about gender, or whether you identify with a more feminine or masculine style of leadership, the goal here is to create equilibrium in how we show up as leaders. Each chapter will highlight one of the 7 Feminine Strengths and 4 Masculine Strengths from the FLM that can help women become better leaders. These capacities, if fully incorporated, can help you cultivate a leadership style that is effective in leading teams and building an inclusive culture. So let's get started!

CHAPTER 4
Vision

Set a Clear Intention and Communicate a Compelling Message

It's well known that one of the most important qualities in any leader is vision, which is why it's the first strength featured in the FLM. But it's not just about having vision—you might have the best idea on earth, but if your team isn't inspired by it or doesn't even know about it because you haven't taken the time to communicate it, I've got news for you—your big idea isn't going anywhere. Or you might be too focused on the vision and your excitement about it, but forget to delegate the details. There are typically two different ways leaders vision—through seeing the big-picture or being more of a detailed thinker, so let's start by looking at what I mean by that.

Big-picture thinkers are those who are able to zoom out and get a bird's-eye view of where they want to go. These types of people are blue-sky thinkers—they are not constrained by practicalities or even logic. They come up with big ideas, which most often times can be game changers. Big- picture thinkers tend to get very excited about their idea and like to jump into quick action. The sky is the limit for these folks, and they can be very inspiring to be around because of their fresh new ideas and ability to think big. However, when it comes to execution they have difficulties in delegating and setting attainable, actionable goals. Although they can inspire and get people on board, they can miss the boat when it comes to strategic thinking and execution.

Detailed thinkers are the opposite of big-picture people. They like to think of all the steps it will take to get to the end goal. Although they might seem like skeptics, their ability to pay attention to detail also helps them predict potential pitfalls. Strategic thinkers at their core, they can put actionable steps in place that pave the way for achievable results. However, when it comes to communicating the bigger vision, detailed thinkers tend to forget that important step. They are so focused on the minute details, they fail in communicating the big-picture to the team, leaving them in the dark much of the time, which leads to confusion as well as a lack of motivation and engagement.

When leading a project, a group of people, or an organization, we have to be sure to take the time to properly convey our vision. As women leaders, it's important to do this in a way that is inspiring and compelling. In order to do this, we must first identify which camp we fall into. Take the quick quiz below to determine whether you are a big-picture thinker or a detailed thinker.

What Type of Thinker Are You?

Exercise #6

1. How often do you take time to communicate your vision to your team or customers?

   a. Often

   b. Sometimes

2. Is it difficult or challenging for you to communicate your message? If so, why?

   a. I don't have a problem with this.

   b. Busy executing the details or just too busy.

3. Would you describe yourself as someone who:

   a. Has lots of big ideas, is creative, and gets easily excited and passionate about her ideas.

   b. Likes to get the job done, would rather work alone, executes the details, and delivers results.

4. Do you take the time to address concerns and make sure everyone is on board with your vision or the company's vision before forging ahead?

   a. Yes

   b. No

5. Do you tend to get too mired in the details and strategy on how to execute a project or plan?

   a. No

   b. Yes

If you answered mostly *a*, then you are probably a big-picture thinker. You take the time to communicate your vision clearly, but may not always set clear expectations and a roadmap on how to get there. If you answered mostly *b*, you're a detailed thinker, and you'd rather just get the job done and then worry about getting other people on board. If you fall in the middle, then congratulations, you are probably pretty balanced in this area!

Once you've determined if you are a big-picture thinker or a detailed thinker, the next step is to think about the desired impact you want to have. Is your goal to motivate and inspire your team to follow your vision? Or is it to execute flawlessly on a strategic plan? You can't have one without the other; as a leader your job is to inspire your people into action *and* be clear in your expectations, delegate effectively, create accountability, and deliver results. But depending on whether you are a bigpicture thinker or a detailed thinker, this may not come as easily or naturally as one would think.

If you are a big-picture thinker, once you've communicated your grand vision it's important to follow through with clearly set expectations, roles, responsibilities, direction, and delegation. Unfortunately, many women find it difficult to do this and instead take on too many tasks. We often grapple with that pesky voice that says "Shouldn't I be able to do all of this by myself?" or "I don't want to bother someone else with this, I'll just take care of it." Or worse yet, we micro-manage and become too heavily involved in all the details. Either way, it can have detrimental impact on you and your team's productivity and performance.

Once you've identified if you're a big-picture thinker or a detailed thinker, take a moment to reflect on how you communicate your vision. Do you tend to skip that very important step when you're launching a new idea, product, or service, or executing on a strategy? How much time do you take to craft a compelling message, one that communicates your message clearly, and is inspiring so that your team wants to jump on board? Or do you tend to hold back your message all together?

Being Assertive

Assertiveness, one of the Masculine traits I've identified as part of the FLM, has become a buzz-word for women. For example, take Sheryl Sandberg's *Lean In*, where she encouraged women to speak up, be more ambitious, not sit in the back of the room and instead take a seat at the table. All this is well and good advice, and I completely agree that we can help close the gender gap by taking this strategy. But here's the catch—being overly assertive or aggressive in your style can have the opposite impact. Taking over the conversation or bulldogging isn't going to help with your likeability factor. In fact, according to *Women and the Labyrinth of Leadership*, verbally intimidating others can undermine a woman's influence, and assertive behavior can reduce her chances of getting a job or advancing in her career. Essentially, when women are overly aggressive, it works against them. So how can we be assertive and speak our minds without alienating others?

The solution is learning to be assertive and at the same time making sure you lean into the other qualities of the FLM. For instance, before you jump to a conclusion about someone and point the finger at them, or act defensively, why not practice empathy by putting yourself in their shoes? Maybe ask questions and get curious to find out whether your assumptions are correct. This can lead to dialogue instead of one-way conversation that often can feel like we are blaming the other person.

Or what if you have an idea that you really want to express, yet you find that you often hold yourself back instead of speaking up? You can move into vulnerability, and allow yourself to take that risk by voicing your opinion or idea. If people don't like it, then you can practice being resilient and let it just roll off your shoulders instead of taking it personally. These are just some ways you can leverage the different qualities of the FLM to develop an assertive style that is both impactful and effective.

Tips on How To Build a Compelling Message To Convey Your Vision

Here are a few tips that can help you achieve balance so you can be both a visionary thinker and a flawless executor, regardless of whether you fall in the big-picture camp or the detailed camp:

1. Think about your vision—what excites you about it? How is it different, what is unique about it? What are the potential outcomes or how will it impact the business or your stakeholders?

2. Create an outline of your idea and vision, along with the attributes you came up with from Question #1.

3. Practice delivering the message in front of the mirror. Take a minute to center yourself, to connect with the excitement you feel about your vision, and speak from a place of truth. Don't worry about getting it perfect, just speak from your heart as if you were talking to a dear friend. Practice this until it comes naturally and where you don't have to think about it.

4. Deliver your message at your next team meeting in person! Don't hide behind an email or a group message. Gather your team together, maybe take them off-site, but find a time to communicate your vision.

More Tips in Delivering Your Message

Ask for input. Even though we believe our ideas are the best, most often they can be better if we allow others to contribute and shape the vision. Allow space for input from your team or your collaborators.

Stay open. You don't have to agree with everyone's idea or even incorporate their ideas. The goal is to make people feel included in the process and be heard. This goes a long way in cultivating engagement and motivation on your team and creates an environment of inclusiveness.

Don't take it personally. If some people on your team don't agree with your vision, try not to take it personally. Listen to and address their concerns. Ultimately you are the leader and get to decide whether their input is valid or not.

Stay humble. If good ideas emerge and it makes sense to incorporate them, well then by all means do so! Don't let your pride or feelings of needing to be right get in the way of good ideas. The best innovation happens when we stay humble as leaders and admit that we don't have all the best idea or answers.

And What about Passion?

What is a vision if it doesn't have passion behind it? What are some of the most memorable speeches of our time? A few that come to my mind: John F. Kennedy's address during the Cuban Missile Crisis, Martin Luther King Jr's "I have a dream" speech or President Barack Obama's address to the nation when he was first elected. When you hear them speaking, can't you just feel the passion in their voices? You could sense that they believed in what they were saying with every fiber in their being. As leaders, we can't be afraid to show our passion for what we stand for. As women, our challenge comes when we hold back because we think it might not be PC, people will get the wrong impression or be put off by what we have to say.

Harnessing passion is an art form in and of itself. If used aimlessly and without thought, it can polarize a room full of people very quickly. It can even be taken as anger or some other negative emotion. As women, we tend to be emotional and passionate—sometimes even when we don't need to be! Acknowledging our passion is OK, and bringing it into the workplace can be good in terms of motivating others and keeping ourselves motivated in the roles we perform. The trick is how do we use our passion in a way that doesn't offend or get perceived negatively by others?

When Rosie Cofre was tasked with leading the Employee Resource Organizations (EROs) at Cisco, she decided she was going to do it a different way. Traditionally EROs are underfunded, and unfortunately aren't tied into corporate strategy or goals, although they are aimed at improving employee engagement and performance. "I knew that for EROs to really make an impact within Cisco, our value had to be tied to overall company business goals."

By advocating from the ground up, Rosie successfully grew participation in the new program from 9% to over 21%. She attributes her success to innovative strategies she describes as "disruptive"—someone who has the courage to think outside of the box and then advocate for those ideas, passionately and consistently. "I still have people who don't like me because they know I'm a disrupter. Many people warned me that I was too forward-thinking, that I was stirring the pot. I stayed true to my convictions, knowing I was doing the right thing to get measurable results that would lead to real change."

The way she reached her goal was through true Feminine Leadership. She had a big and bold vision she was truly passionate about. To bring her vision to life, she took time to develop relationships with key decision makers, getting them on board by clearly explaining her vision for change. On top of that, she wasn't afraid to trust her gut and follow her instincts. "I knew it was the right thing to do, and I stuck with it. I didn't give up although many people told me it would take a very, very long time to realize my vision." She also had support from her female boss, who encouraged her along the way. "I couldn't have done it without Sandy; she was my champion and gave me the strength to move forward."

The other thing Rosie did well was she designed the program in a truly feminine and balanced way. She made sure the objectives of the EROs were aligned with Cisco's overall business goals, setting it up for success. This is one of the biggest challenges of any Diversity & Inclusion initiative, especially those related to gender, but pivotal to ensure success. Rosie also created an internal recognition program to drive participation and reward those who volunteered and managed the EROs, a sure bet that people would take it seriously and stay motivated around the initiative.

Because of Rosie's leadership, diversity and inclusion became a natural by-product of her initiatives without necessarily being part of her main agenda. "Inclusion just happened because of the participative nature of how we positioned the EROs. They evolved from groups based on self-identification to diverse communities most relevant to enabling business strategies and initiatives. This is just another example of how organizations can move the needle on their diversity goals, by creating inclusive environments. My hope is that this can be a disrupter throughout the entire organization, so that we can continue to drive true innovation in our business by creating opportunities for cross-functional collaboration."

Gender Stereotypes

Some of the biggest challenges women face in leadership today are gender stereotypes. As much as we would like to believe we live and play in an equal world, all you have to do is step into a boardroom to see how this is still very real. According to *Women and the Labyrinth of Leadership*, people still associate men with the word "leader," as well as qualities like being aggressive, ambitious and dominant, whereas they attribute more matronly qualities to women, like being friendly, nurturing and caring. It goes on to say that these more masculine qualities are also associated in most people's minds with effective leadership, perhaps because a long history of male domination of leadership roles has made it difficult to separate the leader associations from male associations.

For women, this double bind creates a real challenge and explains why people might be more resistant to women's influence than to men's. For example, in meetings at a global retail company, people responded more favorably to men's overt attempts at influence than to women's. In the words of one of this company's female executives, "People often had to speak up to defend their turf, but when women did so, they were vilified. They were labeled 'control freaks'; men acting the same way were called 'passionate.'"

If women are being penalized because of these unconscious biases, we need to address the larger issues. First, we need to bring awareness about how gender stereotypes hurt women's advancement, their ability to contribute as equals, and their ability to express themselves fully. In the meantime, women cannot buy into these stereotypes themselves, internalizing them, acting as a victim or blaming others. Instead, we can find a different way to speak our minds without being aggressive or dominating, or being weak and restrained. By leaning into our feminine strengths, we can find a better approach.

Dropping Into Your Center

Learning how to positively channel emotions is integral if women are going to be able to fully step into their full leadership capacity. We've seen all too often women being labeled ugly things because of misdirected or misunderstood passion, which undermines our influence and authority. Or worse, we know when we just sit quietly and passively, extroverted people get all the attention and glory. In order to be heard to have maximum impact we must first and foremost learn to ground ourselves. That is the reason why you find the word 'Centered' in the middle of the FLM.

Most of us, both men and women, spend a lot of time in our heads, worrying about the future or thinking about the past; planning who is going to pick up the kids, how you're going to juggle five appointments in one day, what you could have done better in that last meeting—the swirling thoughts go on and on. Add to that our increasingly 24/7-wired lifestyle, and you have a recipe for disaster. We are in fact, cut off from the neck below, completely disassociated from the rest of our body. Most of the time we have absolutely no clue what is going on in this amazingly intricate and complex machine that is our body, which is constantly sending us messages and signals via our emotional and intuitive systems.

For women, this is even more of a threat, because we are, as we saw in the neuroscience data, wired for emotional and intuitive intelligence. But what good is that if we aren't accessing or leveraging it? Women are, for the most part, completely unaware of what their bodies are telling them, cut off from the immense wisdom and information it has to offer. Most of the intuitive information lies in our lower chakras—the third chakra, where our will power lies, and the second chakra, where creativity and sexual power reside. Not only are we cut off from it, we are actively pushing it away because of the negative relationship we've built with our bodies over time. Do you know any woman who is completely 100% accepting of her body, flaws and all?

Because we've developed a negative relationship with our bodies, and because of the negative messaging we get via the media about having to be perfect all of the time, we've built a wall that sometimes seems impenetrable. This has got to change if we are ever to learn how to harness the power of our body's emotional and intuitive systems by learning how to ground, center and accept ourselves.

Becoming more centered takes practice, and like building any muscle, requires repetition. To do so, I recommend practicing the Centering Exercise, developed by one of my teachers, Wendy Palmer, who holds a black belt in Aikido. She teaches

Leadership Embodiment which is about cultivating the capacity to use the body as an instrument to gain more presence and impact. I firmly believe that to become good leaders, we need to use the whole of our vehicle (our body) to build presence, and to be more authentic and confident. Through this simple exercise (and lots of practice), we can align our head, heart, and gut so that we are completely centered and therefore more effective as leaders.

Centering Practice

Exercise #7

Start by sitting straight up in your chair, feet planted firmly in the ground, shoulders back. Close your eyes and take a couple of deep breaths, exhaling in and out. On your third exhale, imagine all your energy sinking through your legs and into the ground, all the way into the Earth. On your next exhale, imagine your energy field creating a bubble in all directions around your body. See if you can give it a color or texture. Then try to expand that bubble, little by little. Go as far as you can. Finally, invite a quality into your body; it can be anything you want a little more of. For example, ease, softness, calm, joy. See what it feels like if you had 5% more of this quality in your being. Sit with this feeling as long as you like. And when you're ready, open your eyes.

This exercise should eventually take you less than 30 seconds and is a calming and centering exercise. This practice triggers our parasympathetic nervous system, which signals our brain to relax. When we are relaxed and focused, it is much easier to deal with the stressors around us, helping make better-informed decisions. The problem is that in today's busy world where we're constantly being bombarded by stressors, our bodies are in a constant fight-or-flight response, with elevated stress hormones being released. Our bodies become accustomed to this unnatural state, which makes us tighten up. As Wendy beautifully exhibits in her workshops, her Aikido training has shown her that in combat scenarios, tensing up is a sure-fire way to land on your back.

The same goes in our lives—when we tense up, we have much less of our resources available to us. By practicing centering and relaxing, we retrain our bodies to a new normal, allowing ourselves to go back to a calm state that gives us more access to our intuition, logic, and reasoning. We can make better-informed decisions, and can better handle our emotions. And as women, that is the key to handling tough situations and coming across as cool, confident, and collected. It's also a sure-fire way to earn respect and get our ideas across in a compelling way.

CHAPTER 5
Vulnerability

Asking for Help Is Not a Weakness

Having grown up in a strict household, my whole world revolved around school and home up to the age of 17, at which point, I sort of woke up. I thought, "Why can't I just be myself?" One day, I decided I'd had enough. I needed independence! I knew my reliance on my parents for food, shelter, and all the nice things girls at my age want to have revolved mainly around money. So instead of staying beholden to my parents, I went out and got my first job as an office assistant.

Finally, I was making my own money and didn't have to ask them for anything. This was true freedom! I began to learn how it felt to be independent, and I loved it. And from that day forward, I decided I would never ask my parents for money and would always rely on myself so that I would never ever be controlled by anyone again.

I continued working all the way through college, moved out, and learned how to support myself. Was it scary and difficult at times? Heck yeah! But at least I could do my own thing, and decide how to live my life on my own terms. Did it piss off my parents to no end? You bet it did! But I didn't care—I was finally free and there was NO turning back!

As I continued to support myself, and became more autonomous and independent from my parents, self-reliance became the norm for me. Eventually it wasn't as scary as it was in the beginning, and it became part of who I was. People saw me as very strong and independent—a real go-getter. I got a job right out of college working in event production and had my own place while most of my friends were still living with their parents. I had money to spend. I loved the feeling of autonomy and not having to rely on anyone for anything. I could just be me, make my own decisions, and live life the way I wanted.

But what I didn't realize at the time was that I was becoming *too* self-reliant. The realities of life and having to survive on my own were taking their toll on me. I prided myself on my strength, but at the same time I was isolating myself from receiving—receiving love, receiving help, receiving care. I sure as hell wasn't going to ask for help, and I was definitely not going to ask my parents. I didn't want anyone thinking I was weak. I needed to prove to them and to the world I could take care of myself.

So I continued to push onward—after a few years of total rebellion and partying like a rock star, I knew I had to reign it in and start taking my career more seriously. And so I did. By the age of 26, I was making six figures, working at a very prominent company in Silicon Valley. My life on paper rocked! But what was going on in the inside was a very different story. I had everything I thought I wanted—except I was lonelier than ever, heavier than ever, and feeling very unfulfilled with life. While my friends continued enjoying their 20s, I had a mortgage to pay, huge responsibilities at work, and mounting stress. I was getting older, and I began thinking how great it would be to find a nice guy and eventually settle down. But I had zero prospects and was too busy with work to go out and meet guys. Plus, I thought all guys were losers anyway—I wasn't going to find a great guy even if I tried.

Needless to say, I was depressed. But it didn't make sense— how could this happen? It would only take me another 10 years to figure out the real reason: *I had closed off myself from receiving.* By showing up as a strong, independent woman, I had shut myself off from others. Not showing my softer side, my feminine side, I put off and intimidated most men. By not opening up and asking for help and not showing any weakness, I had isolated myself from the people I loved the most. I learned that being independent is great, until it stops you from being open and allowing love and connection to flow into your life.

Saying Goodbye to "Proving" Your Worth

I know that my story isn't unique—many women struggle with this. Although women acquired more equality and opportunity as we shattered ceilings, we got there by having to "prove" ourselves, basing all our self-worth and identity on our achievements. Being a self-proclaimed over-achiever, I know what this feels like. Nothing is ever enough—there is always a new challenge, a new obstacle to overcome, a new goal to achieve. In business, many women feel like they have to work harder than men to be recognized for their achievements, and they also tend to take on more busy work.

And as it turns out, all of this has had a pretty negative impact on our happiness. Recent studies show that women's happiness has fallen both absolutely and relative to men in a pervasive way. Women no longer report being happier than men and, in many instances, now report happiness that is below that of men. As more and more women "prove" their value by taking on the world, it seems like we are becoming less and less effective. And we are sacrificing our health and happiness along with it, not to mention our effectiveness as leaders. It has a very real impact on the way we manage and lead others, mainly in the way we delegate, take on responsibilities at work, and put pressure on ourselves to be over-achievers. What are we missing by trying to do it all and not asking for help? Might we be doing a disservice to our employees by not delegating or reaching out and asking for their input, ideas, and feedback? What more could we achieve if we allowed others to help us, or better yet, what types of innovation might come out of more collaboration and less direction from us? What new opportunities or projects are we missing out on by doing it all? And most of all, how are we limiting our visibility and influence as we are busy juggling so much?

I learned the importance of saying goodbye to my need to prove my value when I took on the role to produce that 10,000 person conference I talked about earlier. I knew there was no way I was going to be able to go at it alone; I needed to ask for help. When I did, I realized that being vulnerable and asking for help is a hard pill to swallow for the ego, but it can be one of the most important lessons we learn.

These two experiences, one in my personal life and one in my professional life, taught me that women have a choice on how they show up in life and in business. By thinking we can do it all, we end up being the loser. But by opening up to receiving, whether its help, love, care, advice, support, or anything the universe wants to send our way, we make things a lot easier for ourselves and others. By allowing others to help us, we empower both sides. Showing our weakness is a strength, counter to what we are taught. Sharing our vulnerabilities makes us human, and it's what connects us to one another. Instead of walking around trying to hide it, we can embrace it and use it to our advantage. You have probably already watched Brené Brown's infamous Ted talk on the power of vulnerability, but it's worth watching again or checking out if you haven't. It's a lovely reminder that beautiful connections can take place with others when we are able to let go and be vulnerable.

Trust and Let Go

The other important element about showing our vulnerability is the trust required to do so. As we let go of control and begin to trust more it makes us feel like we're somehow on a roller-coaster, and that we might fly off the edge at any moment. It's a terrifying feeling. The beautiful thing I've noticed in my life is that when we let go and fully trust, magic happens. I was taught this lesson after I left the corporate world and decided it was time for a life adventure. I packed up my bags and moved to Italy, just like that. I went without a job, without much money, and without speaking a lick of Italian. The only person I knew was my sister, Rosy, who was living there studying to become an opera singer, and the guy I was smitten with at the time. I mean, why else would a girl move all the way to Italy?

After a few months, my relationship ended, and I was alone again. Only this time I was in a foreign country, where I didn't have a job or a visa so I could live and work legally. As my holiday visa came close to expiring, I knew I had to move fast if I wanted to stay in Italy. It had always been my dream to live and work in Europe, and this was my chance, so I knew I had to make it happen. Only this time I didn't have the means to "make it happen" in the traditional sense. I needed a miracle.

I put out the intention to find a company that would sponsor me to live and work in Italy. I had only been there a few months and didn't have a huge network. The odds were definitely against me. But I let go of control, trusted the universe, and believed that something would pop up to allow me to stay and live out my European dream.

After spending a few weeks scouring job boards and asking a few people for work opportunities, suddenly I saw something on Facebook posted by a guy I had met at a friend's dinner a few weeks before. It was written in Italian, but I figured out it said something about needing an English speaking intern at his digital PR company. Intern? I was way overqualified. But I sent him a quick email saying I was interested, and we met the next day. After some discussion and negotiation, I was hired to work as a Social Media Manager for a large international brand. The best part—he agreed to sponsor a visa so I could live and work in Italy!

Now, you might say that was just a stroke of good luck. Yes, and no. I definitely got lucky that day, but I believe it was more than luck. I truly think it had to do with how I went about creating the opportunity for myself by setting a strong intention, believing it would happen, and then stepping back, letting go, and trusting. This might sounds a bit like something the late

Dr. Wayne Dyer would say, author of many personal development books, who taught people the power of creating their realities through positive intention. But having the firsthand experience of this in my own life, I'm telling you, this stuff really works!

But it only really works when you're able to be vulnerable, when you're able to soften and surrender to life and not feel like you have to make everything happen by yourself. I could have gone out there and met 100 people and not had the same opportunity fall in my lap. But by staying open to receive, I attracted the perfect job for me in that moment. And that is part of the magic we can tap into. When we sink into our feminine, into openness and vulnerability, and really allow ourselves to live there for a while, anything is possible.

Many years later, this proved true yet again. As I began to open up to life and began healing my heart from all my past wounding, an amazing thing happened. I met my soul mate, Chris. His support, encouragement, and belief in me are what led me to write this book. As I opened up to life, and allowed the universe to work through me, instead of trying to make it all happen by myself, life and work became easier, more fun, more joyful, and filled with grace.

Our Strength Is In Our Softness

Being vulnerable for women requires them to first get in touch with their softness. In the alpha culture we all live and operate in, softness is associated with weakness, and thus women have learned to shun it. Instead, we put value on being and doing it all, giving us a sense of achievement. Learning to tap into the softness of our being, rather than the doing, is a fundamental shift in how we show up in the world. And it can be the biggest gift you give to yourself.

When we harden, we begin to move towards the masculine side of the spectrum, which can backfire on women. In the words of one female leader, "I think that there is a real penalty for a woman who behaves like a man. The men don't like her and the women don't either." Women leaders worry a lot about these things, complicating the labyrinth that they negotiate. For example, Catalyst's study of *Fortune* 1000 female executives found that 96% of them rated as critical or fairly important that they develop "a style with which male managers are comfortable." When I personally experienced softening, my whole world changed. I realized I didn't have to make things happen by myself, instead, I could stay open and allow good things to flow into my life, and in the workplace I could lead my teams in a way that was much more collaborative and effective. I learned that by setting strong intentions, I could more easily manifest those things my heart truly wanted. By softening, I attracted people to me, and it was easier for me to build relationships of trust at work and in life. I was able to tap into my empathy and compassion for others, and thus was able to put myself in other's shoes, which strengthened those relationships. Overall, I became more of myself, more authentic, instead of a person hiding behind a mask of hardness and strength.

It took me another 10 years to embody this more fully, and I think I am still finding ways to soften even now. For some, this might be a life-long practice. Because of the values our society holds to be true, mainly individualism and achievement, we must constantly contend with the temptation to harden. But once you begin to see the fruits of your labor, softness will become a more natural part of you, a piece that was always there and never really left, waiting for you to rediscover it.

Softening Exercise #8

This exercise is designed to help you soften energetically and emotionally. The act of softening is a visceral experience, and it can be acquired through practicing being in this state so that your body learns what it feels like. It is also something that is achieved through choice. We can choose to soften in the moment when our instinct tells us to fight. By softening, we have access to our vulnerability, which allows people to relate to us on a deeper level, and helps build relationships with those we work with. It allows us to ask for help, and it creates a bridge during a time of conflict. This next exercise will help you build the capacity to expand and tap into this state of softness.

First, start by doing the centering exercise you learned in the last chapter. Once you are fully centered, begin to reflect on the meaning of softness you hold to be true. What are your biases (conscious and unconscious) about being 'soft'? Take time to explore this piece and do some journaling about it if you feel compelled to.

Next, ask yourself – what would it be like if I brought in the quality of softness by just 10%? What would be different? How would I show up? Notice the things that come up in your body when you ask yourself this question. Once you're ready—turn up the volume and ask yourself—what would it be like if I brought in the quality of softness by 30%? 50? 70%? Finally, what would 100% look like? Again, notice what happens in your body. Journal on what you notice and what comes up for you in this exercise.

Commit to incorporating softness just by 10% each day or week or month, depending on how easy or hard this is for you. Notice the results you get and your impact on others. Does it become easier to be yourself as you soften? Is it uncomfortable? Does it become easier to get the things you want? Is it easier for others to approach you? How does it impact your leadership style? Notice what shifts for you as you soften more and more each day. Celebrate your achievements as you notice them and continue practicing until you have reached a level you are comfortable with.

Leveraging Vulnerability

Susan was a Marketing Research executive at Disney for nearly a decade—a traditional, conservative company dominated mostly by men, which ironically has a very strong female consumer demographic. Although Susan enjoyed her executive role and function, it wasn't necessarily an easy climb up. Having worked her way up the ladder slowly but surely, she witnessed a lot of competitive behavior among both men and women around her and struggled to find a way to "fit in with the boys" and still keep her femininity and authenticity.

The strategy she chose to lead with was using her gift of building real and authentic relationships. "Instead of emulating the typically male-oriented competitive behavior I saw around me, I decided to be vulnerable and stay true to myself. I love connecting with others so I had an open-door policy—people would stop by, sit on my couch, and open their hearts to me. People confided their business and personal issues; they trusted me and felt like they could come to me with their biggest problems.

"Another approach that really worked for me was to think five steps ahead of others, sort of like playing chess. Instead of getting defensive or engaging in conflict with my colleagues,

I would get my ideas heard by thinking much more strategically. This really helped me get ahead while others either hid under the radar, behind a mask, or resorted to engaging in petty political games." Eventually this strategy paid off, and she was recognized and promoted to VP of Strategy Research, thus being much better positioned to have impact with her work.

Susan's story shows what is truly possible when female leaders dare to be open and vulnerable, even in a very traditional corporate environment. By staying soft and creating a safe space for her teammates to approach her, she won people's trust and confidence. Instead of engaging in petty office politics, she thought of ways to gain more visibility and traction with her managers, which paid off in spades for her career. Susan's choice to firmly root herself in her feminine strengths, to soften and leverage the qualities we often think of as being "weak" or "ineffective," actually had the opposite effect even in a highly masculine culture. And the best part is, that by doing so, Susan was able to do what she was most passionate about— making a difference through her work.

CHAPTER 6
Care

Prioritize Self-Care and Embrace Your Innate Gift

This next chapter is about the Feminine strength of Care—caring for others *and* for ourselves. It's no hidden secret that women are by definition caring and nurturing. We are the bringers of life after all. We are the caretakers of our children, husbands, our parents as they age, as well as our friends, team members, and God knows who else. Women spend a lot of time caring for others, making sure others' needs are provided for. While it's great to know that you can always rely on a woman to get the job done or to go the extra mile, it's also a dou-ble-edged sword. That expectation is almost solely on women; that same expectation does not land as much on men. And as women have stepped into balancing careers and their personal lives, we know that this expectation has created a lot of havoc for some! This chapter attempts to look at how we can create more opportunities for self-care as well as how we can be caring in business without being shuttered by stereotypes.

The Price We Pay

Sheryl Sandberg has said it in *Lean In* and Arianna Huffington has reiterated in her book *Thrive*—women need to learn how to push back when they can and prioritize Self-Care. Easier said than done, as any woman who has carried around a huge brick load of guilt can tell you. But feeling guilty for not doing enough, whether that's spending time with your kids, being a good mother, spending long nights at the office, etc., is doing no one any favors. It's hurting our effectiveness as leaders, as well as our ability to be good wives, mothers, and daughters. The age of the superwoman has to come to an end, and it begins with self-respect and confidence in our abilities and value.

Many women suffer from a lack of valuing their gifts and abilities. Gender stereotypes in the workplace don't make this any easier either. Research shows that working professional women have to work approximately 60 extra days or about three months more to earn the same pay as men. This feeds into our insecurities and creates a belief that if we just work longer hours, take on more work, and do more, we will some-how be rewarded for this good behavior. Not only are we not always rewarded for that extra work, what has evolved over time is that women value themselves based mostly on their accomplishments and what they have achieved, instead of their gifts and abilities. We have become a nation of over-achievers, and women are leading the charge.

Unfortunately all this overachieving has not led to more happiness as one would expect. It's also not led to more women in leadership positions. Instead, it's led to a lot of burnout, depression, and illness. In fact, we are more burned out and depressed than ever before, and it's been shown that Type-A personalities (people who are driven and competitive), as well as those who have higher expectations of work and life, experience more burnout. In comparison, men are 25% more likely to take breaks throughout the day for personal activities, 7% more likely to take a walk, 5% more likely to go out to lunch, and 35% more likely to take breaks "just to relax." So why do we continue to behave in the same ways that lead us to undesirable results?

Women Can't Have It All, Sorry Ladies

All of this is telling us that we need to start with ourselves. It's all well and good to be nurturing and caring, but if we don't care for ourselves, it becomes really hard to care for others. My belief is that women are too stressed out, too overwhelmed, and too burned out to care. It's hard to show up with a smiling face when you are running on a few hours sleep and worried about who is going to pick up your kids from school. It's hard to care about your kid's homework or how they are doing at school when you have a pile of work that needs to get done at the office. It's hard to delegate or develop your employees through coaching or mentorship if you're constantly burdened with busywork, or just plain tired.

Let's face it—being the modern career woman isn't all that it's cracked up to be. Unless you are like the CEO of Yahoo, Melissa Meyer, and can build a nursery for your kids next door to your office, the realities of being a working mom are pretty harsh. And to top it all off, as a culture of overachievers we expect to be perfect at it all. Ladies, women can't have it all, at least not all at once. Ann Marie Slaughter points this out in her now famous 2012 *The Atlantic* article, "Why Women Still Can't Have It All."

And it's OK that we can't have it all. Because it isn't fair (I have a value around fairness!). Men are not burdened with the same things we are. They don't have to go through 9 months of pregnancy, hormonal roller coasters, or breast-feeding. Men aren't always expected to do all the house chores, shopping, cooking, cleaning, and laundry. Men aren't always there to pick up the kids from school, or make sure the homework is done, or even there to put the kids to sleep. But women are, for the most part, still expected to be there for all those things and more. And now with the technology age, we are also expected to be on call 24/7 to respond to work-related emails. Is this really sustainable? Who are we kidding here? Or better yet, what are we trying to prove?

Since the feminist movement, women have been in a fight to prove they can do it all, and have given it their all in the quest for equality. In my opinion, modern women are still stuck in that fight and can't seem to extract themselves from it. We want to have meaning and purpose through our careers, *and* want to be amazing mothers, bring up amazing children, *and* to be wonderful wives to our husbands. But we are failing at it, and failing miserably and projecting this onto our children. An alarming sign of this can be seen in the recent string of teenage suicides that took place, which some kids attributed to too much adult pressure. This happened in Palo Alto, CA, a highly affluent and extremely Type-A town in the center of Silicon Valley. It's clear that our children are suffering, either because of not enough interest and time put into their upbringing, due to both parents working highly stressful jobs, or because of the high-stakes pressure parents are putting on their children to succeed and overachieve.

If we want to end this vicious cycle, we have to be the trail-blazers in finding alternative designs for our lives and careers that are more sustainable, collaborative, and truly equal. The first step in this is to have open dialogue around what's not working, and then work together (men and women alike) to create solutions that work to support the lifestyles we aspire to. Here in the United States, some of those solutions require leg-islative action, like equal pay, paid maternity leave, etc., which require leadership trail-blazed by women, supported by men. This is in the best interest of both sexes, so it shouldn't just be a "woman's issue." We have to do a better job at inviting men to have that discussion with us, and then lobby those who are in positions of power. Another thing we can do is begin small and start right where we are. Change can start with each of us making different choices every day. Whether it's leaving work early to make it home by dinner or saying no to yet another special project, you will be doing what you are instructed to do every time you board an airplane—first put the oxygen mask on yourself, then on others.

Letting Go of Over-Achieving

I've coached too many women who are either in a career that they are not happy with or are generally overwhelmed or burned out. I've also coached women with children who have left the corporate world to start a business, but are riddled with guilt about leaving their children to attend to their business, and can't manage their time well. Something's gotta give! We have to come to terms with the fact that we will never ever be able to do all of it well. We need to ask for help. I also believe women need to start valuing themselves, start setting more attainable goals, and really assess what is going to make them truly happy.

This same concept applies to leadership too. Too many women make the mistake of taking on too much responsibility to prove their worth and ability. Instead, if women realized they *do* have the ability, they would just *own* it. Once you own your gifts and uniqueness, the need to prove fades away. It becomes easier to make decisions that are better in terms of your own productivity and the productivity of your team or business, which ultimately leads to better results. Women need to learn to be confident and then delegate, instead of being afraid to ask for help or afraid to be seen as weak for doing so. This is a fine line to walk, and I am in no way suggesting you shouldn't stretch yourself, or aim for a seat at the table. What I am saying is that it is about finding a balance that works for YOU, whatever that looks like. It's about being honest and truthful with yourself, your family and your peers, and not feeling unnecessary guilt or like a failure because of your choices.

Resilience

We know that women tend to value themselves based on their accomplishments and hard work, so any perceived failures impact them more negatively. Men don't spend so much time thinking about mistakes or failures they've made, and they certainly don't take it as personally as women do. And therefore resilience and the ability to bounce back from setbacks come naturally for them. This is a masculine trait that is essential for women to master, which is why I've included it as part of the FLM.

Most women think that if they just get that Ph.D., or take more workshops, or work extra hours, only then will they have enough experience and knowledge to go for their dreams. And God forbid there's some sort of failure—that can cost women a lot of overanalyzing and thinking and can even stop some women dead in their tracks. The missing ingredient here is confidence—the ability to turn your thoughts into action. Men seem to have an easier time at this in general, while women hold themselves back time and time again because they don't believe they are good enough.

Again, the antidote to this is to develop resilience through working on improving the relationship you have with yourself. By replacing the constant sabotaging dialogue in your head with reminders of your gifts, talents, experience and knowledge, you can begin to own your value. Concentrating on what you are doing well, instead of what else you could be doing better, can help tame those demons as well. Instead of comparing yourself to others, focus on what unique talents you bring to the table. Learning to shrug off failures or mistakes and not take them to heart is key. Over time as you build your self-confidence, the need to over-achieve will fall away. This will leave you with time and space to pursue projects that you're really passionate about or to create more visibility for yourself through developing strategic relationships, taking on more strategic tasks, and playing a bigger game. Those are the things that will make you feel more fulfilled, and ultimately will help you lead more gracefully.

Take the Long View

Prioritizing yourself is easier said than done, but it is essential if we are to close the gender gap in leadership. Women have to put their foot down and prioritize their well-being and happiness in order to have energy to go the distance. One thing that has helped me in my career is taking the perspective of the "long view." When I was in my 20s and early 30s, I felt like I had to do it all right now. I was driven, had big goals, and worked hard. I was so ambitious that I ended up buying a house at age 26. Nothing like a mortgage to keep you ball-and-chained! By my late 20s I was so alone and stressed out with responsibility, that I knew I had to change something if I ever wanted true happiness. And that's when I had a huge perspective shift about my career and the impact I knew deep down inside that I wanted to have on the world.

Once I gave myself permission to look down the road—5, 10, 15, 20 years, I realized that I had a lot of time to achieve all the things I had my eyes set on. The understanding that I didn't need to have it all right now gave me the freedom to really reflect on what I really wanted my life to look like and what MY values were (not my parents' or what society told me I should want). I set a real intention to find work that was meaningful to me, something which would help others and where I could make a difference. After two years of searching, I found coaching as a profession—it really resonated, and it was aligned with my true purpose. I began taking steps to leave the career trajectory that I was on and start all over, from scratch.

As big and scary a leap as that was for me, I don't think I would have taken it if I had been concentrating only on the here and now. I had to make some tough decisions, but I don't regret a single one I made. I started to trust myself and made decisions based on my values and what felt good to me. And it led me to live in places like Italy, where I had amazing adventures and met many wonderful people, some of whom are still friends to this day. Most of all, I gave myself the permission to find myself and express my voice, instead of living with all the pressure and expectation of others.

So that's something I recommend you reflect on: What would be different if you had a shift in perspective about your work and career? What would you do differently if you took the long view? Take some time to journal about this before you go on.

Create Structures That Prioritize Self-Care Exercise #9

Many of us think that we'll just prioritize self-care and that it will somehow magically fit into our schedules. The reality is that it takes setting the intention and then looking at what you must say NO to, so you can truly create the space for self-care. Here are steps to get you there:

1. How would you rate your level of self-care at the moment, on a scale of 1-10 (10 being you are getting massages once a week, 1 meaning once a year)?

2. If you were at a 10 with your self-care, what would that look like?

3. Now that you know what the optimum place is, come back to the present and go up one level. What does one level up from your current state of self-care look like, and what would be different for you here?

4. What do you have to say NO to in your life to make time and space to get to the next level of self-care?

5. What are you saying YES to by committing to selfcare? What will positively change in your life? (More energy, productivity, time with kids, etc.).

6. What structures or activities would you like to commit to which would help you get to your goal of self-care? (Exercise 3 times a week, meditation daily, massages once a week, etc.)

7. How are you going to create accountability for yourself so you can stay on track? (Buddy system, tell a trusted friend about your goal, ask your husband to keep you accountable, etc.)

Congratulations, you have successfully committed to prioritizing self-care! One way to help keep this momentum is to tell a few key people that you have committed to this, like your boss or manager, your spouse, or even your kids. By communicating the "why" behind your actions, those affected by your absence won't be alarmed or think you're slacking off. On the contrary, they'll probably cheer you on and keep you accountable if they see you going back to your old ways. Now the final step, and this is the hard one—let go of the guilt! You can do this by reminding yourself of #5—what are you saying yes to by committing to self-care? Keep a list handy and refer back to it anytime you feel the guilt creeping in. Positive reinforcement also helps—as you see the positive outcomes of this, remind yourself and celebrate your wins!

Delegation: A Game-Changer

Another antidote to overwork is being able to effectively delegate in order to manage your time better, get more done, and focus on what counts. Whether you run a small business or manage a team of hundreds of people, or even if you are a stay-at-home mom, you need to know how to delegate, and delegate well. But here's the catch: this means letting go of control. Yes, you heard that right—letting go of control. For a self-professed control freak, I will be the first to admit how hard this is to do. And since I have had to work on letting go, I can speak from experience that it can be done and done in a way where you can feel comfortable knowing the end result will be just as good as if you did it all yourself.

The beauty of delegation and finding key partners to collaborate with in any venture or business setting, is that it's a win-win for everyone involved. When we delegate, we empower others to jump in and take responsibility for their actions. We ask them to be more creative, to be more resourceful. We give others a chance to grow and learn and develop useful skills. And best of all, we give ourselves a break from tasks that others can perform so that we can focus on the important stuff.

For many, that could mean focusing on higher-value items, like business development and strategy or building relationships with key partners. Or it could mean more time to focus on your kids or even on your personal life (single ladies, you know what I mean!) The shift in perspective here is that both are valuable and important. We can't continue putting ourselves, our lives, our health, and the well-being of our families at the bottom of the priority list. Just as we can't sacrifice the growth of our business or the growth of our employees. By delegating, we can address all these areas, and excel at all of them.

Now most of you reading this are thinking—"I know how to delegate. I'm a good delegator." Fair enough, but before you let yourself off the hook, I'll just ask you to answer this one question: Do you feel overwhelmed in any area of your life right now? If your answer is yes, chances are you could do a better job at delegating. And as Sheryl points out in *Lean In*, it can start at home with our husbands or partners, making sure they are participating in an equal share of the parenting and responsibilities at home. For this to happen, we have to let go of control and expect that they are going to do it their way. Make peace with that, and stop aspiring for perfection.

As we look at our workplace and the teams we work with—getting really good at delegating means setting clear up-front expectations and creating accountability. When you set people up for success by communicating your expectations, the likelihood that they will succeed is much greater. I say this when coaching many high-level managers and executives who miss the mark on this because of a fear of letting go of control or due to a perfectionism streak (and I see this in both men and women by the way).

The beauty (for those perfectionists out there) of setting clear expectations and creating accountability is that there is much less chance for mistakes. When we take the time to communicate our vision for the deliverable at hand, and clearly indicate what we expect to see as the end result, it makes it easier for the person on the doing end to deliver results. By creating an achievable timeline for this and setting up accountability and checkpoints along the way, we can ensure that the work is being done in a timely manner and in a way that is satisfactory to us. And just like that, all you have to do is oversee things, and be available to troubleshoot or coach people to help them develop the skills they need to do a better job. That is what effective leadership looks like, and it should be something women aspire to, instead of heaping on more tasks that don't earn them promotions, and in most cases, not even the credit they deserve.

Channeling Our Inner Nurturer

Some of the things women have been observed to do more frequently than men are things like acting as role models, being better at setting expectations and rewards, inspiring, participative decisions, as well as coaching and mentoring others. Maybe because we have the nurturing gene, or maybe because we are wired for it, the fact remains that women consistently do these things more frequently. Now it's not to say that there aren't men out there that are also good at any of this stuff or can't develop the skill. But I believe women tend to be naturally caring, and this can be used as an asset in a leadership context.

On the flip side, women have unfortunately been labeled as too caring and therefore have been pigeon-holed into roles like Human Resources, Marketing, or Administration, instead of other strategic roles or careers in STEM (Science, Technology, Engineering and Math) that men typically dominate. Stereotypes describing women as "too nice" or "too sweet" have impacted our perceptions that women aren't made of leadership material. The damage of these biases is so bad that over time women actually began to believe them. Somewhere along the way, being caring or nurturing became a bad thing, so they avoided it like the plague. To divorce themselves from this stereotype, women have skewed to the masculine side of the spectrum and as a result have turned into literal robots—emotionless, overly professional, and stiff. Where's the authenticity in that??

We can begin to change this narrative by bringing in the caring and nurturing side of things into the way we do business. Women have to wake up and look themselves in the mirror and ask if this is who they really are at their core. Ask yourself—what would be different if I were more myself at work? Try it, experiment with it, and see what happens. I dare to say that if you show up even 5-10% more caring, people will notice and respond positively. People are human beings and want to know that their leaders care about them. More and more companies are realizing this fact and implementing programs to impact this type of culture change. Women can lead the way by embracing their inner nurturer and bringing that part of themselves to work.

Secondly, we have to change our view of leadership entirely. We have to make it OK for our leaders to care—whether it's about their people, or the community, or the planet at large. For far too long, companies have cared about one thing: the bottom line. But as we begin to see that our actions have bigger consequences and that we can no longer ignore the human and environmental impacts the actions of big business are having all around us, we need to bring care back as an integral value to business. Women again can be the leaders in this. After all, we are usually the ones who are left to deal with the mess at the end of the day. The actions that are taken by the companies we work for impact all of us. This notion of every man for himself isn't real. We are interdependent human beings, living in a fragile ecosystem that is in serious risk of collapse because of this idea of individualism. Once we accept that care indeed has a place in business and that we can care about our teams, the community, and our environment and still be profitable, we will be one step closer to finding the solutions to our very real, very big challenges.

CHAPTER 7
Intuition

Tap Into Your Wisdom and Trust Your Gut

Another gift women possess that is perhaps one of the most important of the 7 Feminine Strengths featured in the FLM is our gift of intuition. Some might describe it as an inner knowing and other, more spiritually inclined people, might call it a connection to a "Source" or a "Higher Power." Whatever your definition of intuition is, anyone who has ever experienced the whisper of that inner voice knows that it is very much connected to something bigger than yourself. Our intuition or gut instinct seems instinctual, perhaps coming from an ancient evolutionary source. This instinctual knowing lets you decide at lightning speed how you feel about something based on all your past experience as well as all the knowledge and information stored in the depths of your subconscious.

If our bodies are the source of this information, then our emotional system is the channel for communication. Our emotions are sending us signals and are reacting to all the information input it receives in any given moment. For example, think about a time when you received some really good news. How did you react? Maybe your heart started beating a bit faster, you felt happy or ecstatic. All of those emotional and physical reactions were sending you signals as a reaction to the news you received. I like to call this our Emotional Guidance System or EGS for short. It is always there, working in the shadows, sending us information about the things that are happening around us.

Just as how a GPS works on helping us get from Point A to Point B, our EGS can point us to information that can help us reach a decision based on the input we receive. Gut feelings aren't just happening randomly, they are physical sensations that carry meaning, according to Louann Brizendine, MD, in her ground-breaking book, *The Female Brain*. She sites brain scan studies that show the relationship between a woman's gut feelings and her intuitive hunches are grounded in biology. Which explains why women know things about the people around them—they can feel a husband's infidelity or a child's distress at a gut level.

And then, of course, there is the logical and analytical brain that comes into play. Whenever we need to assess a situation or make decisions, we automatically go into our brains to analyze the information coming in. Every day we are encouraged and rewarded for how smart, intelligent, and quick we can be, especially in the workplace. This enforces the belief that logic and analysis trump intuition, which again skews towards the masculine side of the spectrum. The result is that over time, we shut ourselves down from listening to the valuable information that our bodies are trying to tell us. We ignore the immense wisdom that lies in the female body in an attempt to make sense and rationalize the incoming data with our minds. Even Albert Einstein said that "the intuitive mind is a sacred gift and the rational mind is a faithful servant. We have created a society that honors the servant and has forgotten the gift."

Now I'm not saying that using our brain is useless and we should abandon analytical thought. I'm sure Einstein was not suggesting that when he described the rational mind as a faithful servant. What he was implying, and I am suggesting, is that we are missing out on a wealth of data that our intuitive and emotional bodies are sending us at any given moment. How many times have you had a gut instinct and second guessed it? How many times have you not trusted your intuition? How tuned in are you to your emotions and what they might be telling you?

Being a very emotional person myself, I discovered the EGS while going through a particularly stressful time in my life. There was a lot of turmoil, a lot of mixed emotions, and I was really unsure of which way to go. I was getting mixed messages from all my friends and family, and I was just confused. One day, as I was breaking down from all the difficulty, I got the idea to quiet down all the outside voices and just tune into my own body. As I listened, I began to hear what those emotions were telling me. In about five or ten minutes, I understood what was really going on inside of me. Soon I had a sense of clarity, and things weren't so confusing anymore. I felt calm and peaceful for the first time in months. And shortly thereafter, I was able to make some pretty tough decisions and move forward, without having to ask for anyone else's advice on the matter.

Leveraging Intuition Exercise #10

This next exercise is to help you gauge how effectively you're currently leveraging your intuition. Answer the questions below after some reflection:

1. How often do you listen to and follow your gut instincts?

2. What might be holding you back from following your intuition?

3. What might be possible if you were to more fully listen to the guidance of your intuition and trusted yourself?

4. How would you show up differently in a business context if you followed your intuition?

A Missed Opportunity

For us women, tapping into and trusting the wisdom of the body is one of our biggest gifts and points of advantage. Unfortunately, we aren't leveraging it as much as we could. Instead we are muddled in self-doubt, worry, and over-analysis. For those of us who can be too emotional, especially in the workplace, learning how to handle our emotions effectively is essential. If we don't, we can be seen as erratic or unprofessional, and it can greatly undermine our authority. Learning how to listen to our EGS for guidance by dropping into our intuition can be a hugely beneficial tool for women to help them use their emotions wisely.

One of the main reasons I believe women battle self-doubt and are unable to really trust their gut is because of the negative relationship we have with our bodies. Negative self-image prevents us from fully trusting and listening to our intuition. Because our bodies are such a source of angst (I know mine is!), we tend to be in battle with our bodies most of the time. "I need to lose 20 pounds" runs through my head about a 100 times a day. If I'm busy battling with myself to lose that weight, criticizing my body every time, am I likely to listen to what wisdom it has for me? Do you listen to the advice of someone you don't care for? So instead of dropping awareness into our bodies we rely on our powerful minds that often send us into a spiral of self-doubt, limiting thoughts and over-analysis and hindering our ability to make decisions or reach for what we really want. And that is a huge missed opportunity.

Of course you can attempt to address any physical issues with your bodies but unless you turn down the volume on the critical voices in your head, losing those pesky pounds can be that much more challenging, or impossible in some cases. I've personally known people who have lost a lot of weight or have had plastic surgery to correct 'imperfections', but still hung on to their negative body image and low self-esteem. The critical self-talk and dialogue that we choose to engage with can have a pervasive and often negative impact, not just how we view ourselves, but how we judge and value ourselves. Comparing ourselves to others is another downside to this, and it is something I've personally had to overcome, and many of my female clients have also dealt with. The bottom line—unless we address the underlying issues of our critical self-talk, it will not only hurt our self-confidence, but it will undermine our ability to trust our intuition and limit the access to the wisdom our bodies have to offer.

Trusting Your Intuition

Begin to become familiar with the signals your body sends as you honor your values and have your needs met. Learn when things feel good in your body—maybe your energy increases, your heart rate goes up, you feel motivated, or you feel elation. Those are all signs that you are on the right track. Become comfortable with trusting those feelings and sensations—it's your body communicating with you. Try not to overthink or let your rational mind start over analyzing too much. Start with small steps, like trusting your body's signals around less signifi-cant issues, and build trust with yourself that way. As you con-tinue doing so, it will become second nature, and you'll trust those signals more and more.

On the contrary, notice anytime a decision or action doesn't feel good. What does that feel like in your body? Maybe your muscles tense up, you clench your jaw, you get aggravated, or stay awake at night. Again, these are all ways your body is trying to get your attention. It's saying— WARNING, what you're doing might be hazardous to your health! It's amazing to me how many times I myself have ignored those warnings, com-pletely disregarded them. I could have saved myself a lot of heartache and sleepless nights if I had just listened! But our powerful minds take control and find ways to convince us that what we're doing is right, or even worse, we fall under the in-fluence of opinion of others.

Once you begin to listen to your body for clues, you'll find that your dependence on others' advice or guidance will lessen.

You'll begin to be your own best friend, being able to quickly make decisions and take actions based on what is right for you. At the end of the day, only YOU know what's best for you. After all, you're the only one having YOUR unique experience. As well as you think your mom, your sister, best friend or peer knows you, they all have their subjective opinions on how you should run your life or career. Although they might have the best of intentions or even think they know better than you, they still aren't having the exact experience you are. Learn how to trust yourself, your intuition, and your body, and soon you'll be spending a lot less time on the phone listening to others tell you how to live your life or how you should conduct yourself in a business context. You'll spend more time listening to yourself, and that, ladies, is where true confidence lives.

This next exercise is designed to help you listen to the signals your body is sending you, and to learn how to tap into your intuition more fully. This tool is especially helpful any time you feel stuck or need to make any sort of decision. It can help you more easily and painlessly make a decision, instead of ruminating for hours, asking friends or colleagues, and losing sleep, and it is one of the most powerful ways I've found to tap into my body's wisdom.

4-Step Body Wisdom Exercise

Exercise #11

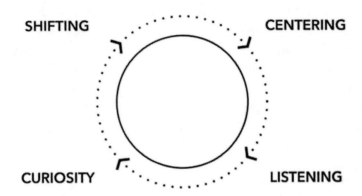

SHIFTING   CENTERING

CURIOSITY   LISTENING

4-STEP BODY WISDOM EXERCISE™

Here is the 4-Step Body Wisdom Exercise™ that I've developed as a simple roadmap to help you drop into your body for answers. This is a great tool to use anytime you may feel stuck or unsure about which way to go regarding a decision, or anytime you feel uneasy or in conflict with something or someone. To utilize this step-by-step tool, think about a situation where you need to make a decision or feel stuck in some way, and then run through these four steps:

1. **Centering.** Practice the centering exercise introduced earlier or start doing some deep breathing to ground and relax you.

2. **Listening.** What sensations or feelings do you notice in your body? Where do you notice tension or heaviness? These are signals or messages your body is sending you.

3. **Curiosity.** What are these signals or messages telling you about the situation? What is the message behind the emotion, feeling, or sensation?

4. **Shifting.** Make a decision or choose an action based on the signal or message. You can now shift out of the feeling or emotion if it is negative or disempowering by choosing a new thought, belief, or action that is more in line with your values. Shift into what intuition and body wisdom are guiding you toward.

What did you notice as you went through the exercise? Do you feel more at ease about the original situation you were thinking of? Do you have more clarity or any new insights? Was this exercise difficult for you? Some may have a very challenging time with this exercise; this is very normal given how cut off we are from our bodies. I do encourage you to try this exercise as often as possible to build the muscle and develop the relationship with your body.

It might take some time, but with practice not only will you have a more positive relationship with your body, but you will be able to make decisions much faster and begin relying on yourself for the answers. This is a very useful tool in the workplace as it will help you be more decisive, less emotional, and a better leader. As you learn to rely on yourself for answers, you will begin trusting yourself more, and as you do this, you will develop more confidence in your abilities. Not to mention all the hours you'll save going back and forth on a decision (or time spent getting advice from others!).

The Confidence Gap

There is more and more evidence that shows that women are less self-assured than men and this directly affects how successful they are. It all begins in childhood—it has been shown that girls are confident up to age 9, but by the time they enter high school there is a steep decline when it comes to self-esteem and self-worth compared to boys, with 46% of boys feeling confident, compared to 29% of girls.

As women enter adulthood, this takes on a myriad of different behaviors. For instance, studies show that men overestimate their abilities and performance, and women underestimate both, although their performances do not differ in quality. Women apply for a promotion only when they meet 100% of the qualifications; men apply when they meet 50%. The natural result of low confidence is inaction as Katty Kay and Claire Shipman state in their 2014 *The Atlantic* article, "The Confidence Gap." They claim that when women hesitate because they aren't sure, they hold themselves back. But when we do act, even if it's because we're forced to, we perform just as well as men do. Taking a hard look at this data, it's not hard to see how the lack of confidence is one of the biggest threats to women's advancement. Not only do we need to recognize it, we need to do something about it.

There is a popular belief among women that they will be promoted based on their level of competence, and the hard truth is that it's just not enough to be competent. Kay and Shipman go on to talk about how confidence matters more than competence when it comes to who is admired, listened to, and who has more sway in discussions and decisions. What studies have found is that it's *confidence* that influences people. Studies show that those who project confidence are more respected. And it also explains why someone less competent is often promoted over someone who is qualified. Think about it—when you listen to someone speak—who do you tend to believe more? Someone who speaks from well-prepared notes or someone who speaks authentically from the heart with confidence? It's confidence and the authenticity that sells, and it pays off in dividends for those who embody it.

So what is confidence? According to Richard Petty, a psychology professor at Ohio State University who has spent decades focused on the subject, "confidence is the stuff that turns thoughts into action." When we as women aren't confident, we hold ourselves back. We don't act, we don't speak up, we hesitate to reach for a promotion because we don't think we are prepared enough or we don't have a degree or enough experience. This comes from a deep-seated fear of failure or a fear of being called out, and in fact many women have the 'imposter' syndrome. You might be familiar with it— it's that pesky little voice that tries to convince you that you aren't qualified enough, and how dare you try to be an expert and speak up in front of everyone else who is much more qualified than you? If this sounds like you, ask yourself this: what would you do if you weren't afraid to fail?

Women must find a way to tackle self-confidence issues if they want to excel in leadership of any kind. But this is easier said than done. Our minds have powerful thought-programming that is reinforced by negative messaging in the media, gender stereotypes, and unconscious biases that keep women believing they are just not good enough. The alpha culture we live in supports and perpetuates this, starting from our classrooms all the way to the boardroom, rewarding those that are extroverted and can show their confidence and leadership ability. This can work against women in a big way, creating an ocean of a divide between those who get ahead and those who eventually check out.

Rebuilding Our Confidence Is Essential To Our Success

One of the remedies to building self-confidence and self-esteem is to heal and improve the relationship we have with our bodies and ourselves. We can do this through self-acceptance. We can do this through building integrity with ourselves. And we can do this by learning to quiet the negative self-talk constantly running in our heads, the voice that says you aren't good enough or is constantly criticizing you. Unfortunately, this is another area where we are much worse than men. We are much quicker to criticize our appearance than men are to criticize theirs. According to one study, 90% of women want to change at least one thing about themselves; 81% of ten-year-old girls are afraid of being fat. And one of the saddest statistics: only 2% of us actually think we are beautiful.

Turning down the volume on our sabotaging thoughts and turning up the volume on our intuition takes practice, and it can be an effective tool in combating a lifetime of negative conditioning. By leveraging this important quality of the FLM we come back into balance with an integral part of ourselves. When we work with our thought patterns and beliefs, and strengthen the relationship we have with ourselves, we can live happier and more fulfilled lives, and most importantly, it will translate into increased confidence in both leadership and in life.

I have seen this formula work time and time again, not only in my personal and professional life, but also in the lives of my clients. Now I'm not claiming that this transformation will happen overnight, nor do I promise overwhelming confidence and joy at all times. It's unrealistic to think that we can eliminate all of our negative thoughts or expect that new ones won't pop up along the way. But learning how to develop resilience and bounce back quickly when we notice those limiting beliefs creeping in, can allow for our intuition to guide us toward decisions that are more aligned with our values and is a way more realistic and reachable goal.

Building Confidence Through Self-Acceptance

Exercise #12

Step 1. Begin to notice each time you choose to think a negative thought about yourself, your body, or your image. Keep a tally of each hurtful thought or belief. Keep this practice for one week.

Step 2. Every time you notice a negative thought, replace it with a more loving and positive thought. Keep a tally of how many times you were able to do this in a week.

Step 3. Create a positive affirmation that helps anchor who you really are. An example of this could be "I am perfect just as I am" or "I am happy, healthy, and whole." Write this on a post-it note and put it somewhere visible. Make this your go-to statement whenever you feel yourself going into a spiral of doubt or negativity.

Step 4. Focus on your positive qualities—make a list of all the things that make you amazing and unique. Better yet, ask people who know you really well to give you a list of positive attributes. Focus on those qualities each day and remind yourself of them when you find yourself going down a path of self-criticism.

Being Decisive

The next Masculine trait in the FLM is being decisive. When we begin listening more closely to our intuition, decisions become much easier to make. In the workplace, this is something that men actually do better than women, which is maybe why it was described as a masculine quality in *The Athena Doctrine* study. Men tend to be much more decisive—they are much more willing to take risks and throw something out there, no matter the outcome. Women tend to be more reserved when it comes to taking risks, which by the way, isn't always a bad thing. I often wonder if the stock market crash of 2008 could have been prevented if there were more women running the financial world! Regardless, women can benefit from being more decisive and taking risks. And they can do this much more gracefully and even more effectively than men who just throw ideas out which may or may not have merit, by tapping into the wealth of wisdom that resides in our intuition.

For instance, you might be interviewing someone who has all the credentials on his resume, and it makes logical sense that this person would be right for the job. But upon meeting him, you get an intuition that they might not be the right fit after all. All logic, according to what the job description states, tells you otherwise. Everyone else in your department who met him thinks he would be great. There's nothing wrong with him after all! But deep down inside, there is a little whisper telling you to keep looking. If you were aligned with your intuition, you would heed those signs, no matter how contrary to logic it sounds, and continue the search.

One way to becoming more decisive is to start building more integrity with yourself by listening to your intuition more closely and getting in tune with its whispers. Begin with baby steps by taking actions based on what your heart and gut tell you. Observe the outcome. Each time you do, you'll be building back the trust that was once broken from all the times you didn't heed those whispers. After repeated practice, you'll notice that you'll trust yourself more and have much less doubt—all roads leading to more confidence and ease.

Integrity Is More Important Than You Think

Many of us underestimate the huge importance of integrity; standing in integrity with yourself, being aligned with your values, and expressing yourself in a way that feels true to you. As you begin to listen to your intuition, you can rebuild the relationship of trust with yourself and in turn strengthen your self-esteem and self-confidence. When you do the opposite of this, you fall out of integrity, which leads to more self-doubt and lack of confidence. It's a vicious cycle but it can be turned around through awareness and a concerted effort to stand more firmly in your own integrity.

In order to tap into your intuition you must build back the trust with yourself. Think about the work and time it takes to build trust with someone who has betrayed you or hurt you in some way. The same goes for yourself—the years of negative self-talk, self-criticism and even receiving criticism from others has the same damaging effect. You betrayed yourself each time you chose to believe those hurtful thoughts. You betrayed yourself each time you didn't listen to your gut, or when you chose to listen to other's advice when making decisions about your life instead of listening to your gut. To undo all that, you can begin with choosing positive and loving thoughts to rebuild a positive relationship with yourself.

CHAPTER 8
Empathy

Put Yourself in Others' Shoes

Empathy comes next in the FLM because it's one of those natural gifts women bring to the table that is mostly underutilized. Women have an amazing gift to listen and listen deeply—we somehow can read between the lines, tap into our intuition, and feel another's pain, sorrow, anger, or other emotions. We are great advice givers and tend to always be there when our

friends need a shoulder to cry on. But where I think we sometimes miss the mark, and this goes for men as well, is being
able to communicate from a place of empathy.

Having empathy and communicating empathically are two
different things. The first is emotional; the second requires action. It's how we communicate with one another that either
leads to conflict or to understanding. The way we express
ourselves is an action, and many times it can have the desired
impact or sometimes an undesired impact. Most of the time
when challenged with conflict, our fight-or-flight mechanism
kicks in and gets us to act defensively, to protect ourselves as
part of a self-preservation mechanism. It's really habitual and
happens at the speed of light on a very subconscious level.
But every time we defend or blame others, we are closing the
window on connection. Nurturing the connection in any relationship is fundamental to being able to work together toward
a common goal—an essential piece of a leader's repertoire of
skills.

The Science Behind Empathy

Simply defined, empathy is the ability to recognize and understand the situation, feelings, and motives of another. When
conveying empathic emotion, we can better understand what
others are feeling, can actively share emotions with others, and
can passively experience the feelings of others. Recently one
of the leading researchers in neuroscience, Marco Iacobini,
found a set of "mirror neurons"—cells that seem to map one
person's actions into another's brain—a kind of imprinting
that explains why role models and mentors can be such powerful influences. "Today we're exploring new frontiers of the

brain—and we're now seeing how humans actually connect in profound ways," says Iacobini. "These insights can completely change the way we think of leading and learning."

"Mirror neurons seem to be a bridge between our thinking, feeling, and actions—and between people," says Iacobini. "This may be the neurological basis of human connectedness, which we urgently need in the world today." In Iacobini's eyes, connectedness could be one of the single most important drivers of change in our time. And there is emerging data to show us that empathy and connection can drive performance in business, in education, and in other sectors.

In schools, where empathy tools are used as part of the education system, students are happier and better adjusted. What may be a surprise is that social and emotional learning programs significantly improve students' academic performance as well. Additional research also shows that emotional intelligence is strongly linked to staying in school, avoiding risky behaviors, and improving health, happiness, and life success. So how does it translate into business? It's been shown that when leaders are trained in "emotional intelligence," (in other words, the skills to work effectively with people) there are fewer accidents; stress is less of a problem, customers are more satisfied, and people become better leaders (just to name a few of the benefits). What may be a surprise is that they also make more money. According to Tony Schwartz, CEO of The Energy Project, "The inescapable conclusion: it pays to care, widely and deeply."

Conflict—How To Embrace It Instead of Running Away

Many women (and men) struggle with channeling and expressing their emotions in the right way, although we are highly emotionally intelligent beings. Women tend to be more in tune with their emotions, they like to talk about their emotions to make sense of them, and many don't have a problem saying how they feel. However, some women do have a real fear of being in conflict with others. They tend to seek harmony and balance, and so it is natural that we run away from even the slightest bit of disharmony. You might disagree with another's point of view or see some sort of transgression that's happening to someone (or to yourself), but instead of pointing it out or speaking up, you keep it to yourself. Or even worse, you might gossip about it with others, thinking you're doing something about it. This is just another example of not standing in integrity with yourself, and over time it can lead to lack of self-confidence and can actually do a lot of damage as it relates to your career and leadership ability.

Now I'm not suggesting you go out and pick fights with everyone you disagree with, or be overly aggressive just to be heard. Unfortunately, women sometimes end up on the masculine side of the spectrum, emulating men in their communication style. This is where gender stereotypes and the double bind come in and create an uneven playing field for women. Men can act aggressively and get away with it more often, whereas women are dubbed "bitchy" or "bossy" when they speak up. But there is a way around this, and it can be done through development of communication skills and through channeling our emotions in the right way. This is an integral skill for women to be able to navigate gender bias in a way that shatters stereotypes and also allows us to have the impact we desire without having to emulate men and without the nasty labels!

How To Deal With Conflict

There are universal needs and values that all human beings need to survive, be happy, and fulfilled. And each of us has a unique roadmap of values and needs, like how our DNA is specific to just us. For example, I highly value autonomy and independence, along with a need for community and connection. You might have a need for fairness and justice, or appreciation and recognition. Each of us has our own set of values and it's very helpful to take some time and examine which values are important to you, as it can help you communicate better and can also help in things like making decisions and channeling emotions. When we are honoring our values, our needs are being met.

For example, when I honor my value of autonomy, I'm meeting my need for personal space and time for reflection. When I am not honoring my value of autonomy, I'm making choices that do not give me time to take personal space for reflection. This leads to me feeling closed in, suffocated or pressured. My body starts sending me signals, for instance, I might become irritated or angry. This is my body's way of letting me know something is awry. If I listen closely to what my body is telling me, I might begin to notice this pattern and realize that it's just my body's way of reminding me to get more personal space so I can reflect, thus adhering to my values. I might do this by asking my husband for some alone time, or scheduling times where I can go to take yoga class or do something on my own. It's a fundamental need that I have to function and be happy, so if I'm smart, I'll honor that value of mine and get that need met. If not, watch out! You don't want to be in my way when that happens, ask my husband!

Below you'll find a list of universal needs and values—take a minute to reflect on which ones are the most important to you. As you become more attuned to your emotions and the messages your body is sending you, you can identify the values that are being stepped on when you feel triggered. Anytime we feel defensive or feel a strong emotion, it means we are being triggered. We tend to go immediately to blame, and point the finger to the other person for making us feel that way. That can lead us to act in aggressive and yes, sometimes in bitchy ways. If we can find a way to understand WHY we are feeling the way we do, by looking at which of our values is not being met in that moment, we can begin to take responsibility for our emotions. If you feel in conflict with something or someone, you can go·back to your list of values to ask yourself why you are feeling a certain way. It's one of the first steps in being able to communicate from a centered and grounded place. It's also one of the most important things we can do to channel our emotions in a constructive way when asking for what we need, in overcoming situations of conflict, or when delivering difficult feedback.

List of Universal Human Needs and Values

CONNECTION

acceptance
affection
appreciation
belonging
cooperation
communication
closeness
community
companionship
compassion
consideration
consistency
empathy
inclusion
intimacy
love
mutuality
nurturing
respect/self-respect
safety
security
stability
support
to know and be known
to see and be seen
to understand and be understood
trust
warmth

PHYSICAL WELL-BEING

air
food
movement/exercise
rest/sleep
sexual expression
safety
shelter
touch
water

HONESTY

authenticity
integrity
presence

PLAY

joy
humor

PEACE

beauty
communion
ease
equality
harmony
inspiration
order

AUTONOMY

choice
freedom
independence
space
spontaneity

MEANING

awareness
celebration of life
challenge
clarity
competence
consciousness
contribution
creativity
discovery
efficacy
effectiveness
growth
hope
learning
mourning
participation
purpose
self-expression
stimulation
to matter
understanding

The Art of Empathic Communication

Communicating from a place of empathy is essential, if not the single most important tool both men and women can learn to improve their leadership and to build positive relationships with each other—from marriages to friendships to boss-employee relationships and everything in between. Sadly, the current system we are operating in has not yet grasped the importance of this skill set and we are not taught to communicate in this way. And the more we drift away from practicing empathy in our daily lives, the more we find ourselves in conflict, both on a personal level and on a global scale.

If we take the premise that any and all change starts with ourselves, then learning the art of communicating empathically could actually change the world. If every single person learned how to do this, I honestly believe we'd have much less conflict—from wars between countries to petty arguments between couples. That is why I believe so strongly in the work of Marshall Rosenberg and his technique of Nonviolent Communication. I teach this tool to all of my clients, and I like to call it "Empathic Communication." It is essentially a basic tool of communication used any time there is a disagreement or charged emotion between two parties.

This tool is also handy in delivering sticky feedback to someone, whether to an employee or your boss, or when you are triggered and feel a strong emotion. Many of us struggle with giving feedback or communicating our needs without blame. Learning to do so is important because as leaders we have to help others grow, so it's a good skill to have if you're tasked with developing or managing people. We also have to learn how to express ourselves in effective ways, so we can deliver our point and get it across. This is one of the most important steps to gaining influence in a business setting, and to garner respect from your peers. It's also a handy negotiation tactic and it can transform your effectiveness drastically. It comes in handy when talking to your husband, or to your kids for that matter. Using this technique makes it a joy to give feedback because more often than not, the reaction is positive and leads towards quick resolution of problems or conflict before it becomes too late.

Before I introduce it, I just want to warn you that this tool is deceptively simple. There are just four steps in practicing empathic communication, but each step is important in its own right. Miss one step, and you're back on the path of blame and arguing. So I coach my clients who are learning this for the first time to practice first by going through each step and writing it down, practice saying it out loud a few times, and then practicing some more before actually delivering it out loud to the person you're in conflict with or when offering feedback. The reason for this is that we are so conditioned to use "blame" language that speaking this way is actually really foreign to most of us. Our autopilot language isn't used to expressing in this way. Practice makes perfect, but expect you will make mistakes along the way. But the more you use it, the more natural it will become, and the less you'll have to work at it.

The Steps to Empathic Communication

Exercise #13

As I mentioned earlier, the steps to empathic communication are simple. I'll introduce them next and then give you an example of how it could be used in an actual conflict situation.

I would highly recommend the book by Marshall Rosenberg, *Nonviolent Communication*, for more in-depth information on this tool. But here is a quick summary so you can begin using this with the key relationships in your workplace and in life. Believe me, your peers and your spouse will thank you!

Step 1. State the observable facts: This is where you say what has happened without your own evaluation of it, only stating facts that everyone can agree on (like evidence you'd submit in court).

Step 2. Describe how this made you feel: These are the feelings and emotions you experienced in that scenario.

Step 3. Explain the values or needs behind your feelings: This is the WHY behind your feelings. Here is the opportunity to explain your values and why you felt the way you did.

Step 4. Make a request for a different action or behavior: An opportunity to dig deeper and understand why the other person behaved the way they did, or to simply request they do a different action next time.

All this sounds fairly easy, right? Trust me, it looks simple, but again, we are not taught this stuff in school, folks. This is usually what we do instead:

1. Feel the emotion—anger, frustration, sadness, etc.

2. Blame the other person for our feelings.

3. Tell the other person what to do to prevent them from making us feel like that next time.

4. Defend, blame, and argue some more.

See the difference? I'll give you an example of a scenario to help you visualize it. Let's say you manage a team of people, and Larry has failed to deliver the report on time for the umpteenth time. You have politely asked him to be timelier, you've given him warnings, you've even talked to him sternly, and still no change. You are fed up and angry, and during a team meeting you lose it in front of your team and bite his head off. Afterwards, you sheepishly call him into your office and half apologize, garnering resentment and disappointment because you know it's not going to change anything.

Now, here is how the conversation could go if using the steps of empathic communication:

1. State the observable fact:
   Larry, I've noticed that this is the tenth time you've been late with the accounting report, which makes it impossible for our team to deliver our numbers to headquarters on time.

2. Describe how this made you feel:
   I'm feeling confused and frustrated, because we've talked about it before.

3. Explain the values or needs behind your feelings
   I have a need around timeliness and hitting our deadlines, and I have a responsibility to deliver numbers to headquarters on time.

4. Make a request for a different action or behavior
   Would you be willing to tell me if there is a reason for your behavior or discuss this with me so we can figure out how to mitigate it?

At this point, Larry might tell you that he has been taking care of his wife and child while she has been ill for the past year, making it difficult for him to appropriately hit his deadlines. Although he should have come forward and shared this fact with you, he was afraid it would impact his professional advancement. So all along you just assumed he was lazy and unreliable. But hearing his point of view has now changed your view of him, and you're no longer angry. You continue to talk about ways to get him team support or brainstorm ideas on how to create efficiencies that will make his work-load easier. No resentment, no embarrassment for Larry, and the accounting report is on its way to being delivered on time.

Now you might be thinking that sounds too easy. But I challenge you to try this next time you're in conflict with someone. Before you jump to a conclusion or make an assumption about the other person, ask yourself, what do I know about this person or their situation? Am I making up a story, or do I have facts to back up my premise? Put yourself in the other's shoes and imagine how they might be feeling. Refrain from creating stories about them, and find out the facts. And most of all, take responsibility for your feelings and reactions, instead of jumping to blame.

Every Action and Reaction Is a Choice

One of the pitfalls in using this tool is that most people forget to do Step 3 (stating our needs/values) and jump right to Step 4 (the request). The reason for this is that most of us are used to saying how we feel, pointing the finger, and then demanding that the other person change. This only leads to a breakdown in communication and leads to nowhere. But when we take full responsibility for our feelings by voicing the need and value behind it, it's like taking that finger and pointing it back to ourselves. This concept might be revolutionary to some—the notion that no one person can make you think or feel anything.

We all have a choice as to how to react to someone's actions toward us. I might react badly to Larry's tardiness, but Jane, who doesn't have the same value around timeliness, just might let it slide. It's all subjective. So by realizing that we react based on whether or not our values are being met, it makes it easier to see how we are in the driver's seat of our reactions. We are constantly choosing, albeit subconsciously, our reactions—no one is doing anything to us.

To help you with this, refer back to the List of Universal Needs and Values. Make a copy of it and keep it handy. When you're practicing your steps of Nonviolent Communication it will help you figure out which values are being triggered, and by doing so you'll understand why you're reacting the way you are which will make it easier to communicate Step 3.

Leveraging Resilience

Another theme I find with many of my women clients (even the senior executives) is a tendency to take any slightly negative feedback personally. As we discussed, women tend to have a very thin shield of protection as it relates to our self-worth and self-esteem. Any sign that we didn't nail it absolutely right can cause worry and self-doubt. We tend to take failures and mistakes closer to heart than men do, and it takes us longer to recover and bounce back from those perceived setbacks. This is just another reason to work on building confidence as well as learning how to not take things personally and being able to bounce back quickly if we do make a mistake.

From personal experience, I can attest to how devastating this can be to your forward momentum. In my career I have let perceived failures or mistakes stop me dead in my tracks.

In some cases it's taken me years to get over it and find the strength to carry on. As I've worked on this (and believe me it's still a work in progress), I've learned that my flaws are actually opportunities to learn from and develop myself and my leadership. My need for perfection and to be liked by everyone has had to take a back seat. Trust me when I say, it is so liberating when you stop caring what the world thinks of you. Accept the fact that you're going to disappoint some people, and that they tend to move on much quicker than you think.

Being resilient has everything to do with practicing self-acceptance. When we can accept ourselves as is, including our bodies for that matter, it becomes less important what other people think. We can learn from our failures and mistakes, instead of letting them hold us back. We can do this by caring about ourselves enough to have compassion even when mistakes are made. However, most of us are so busy self-criticizing and putting ourselves down for every little thing—no wonder we can't handle feedback! Think about it this way—if your friend or loved one made a mistake, would you berate them or call them stupid? Probably not, right? Yet we don't hesitate to put ourselves down any time we think we've failed. This self-torture needs to stop, and instead we can learn to treat ourselves with the same compassion we use towards people we love.

Practicing Self-Empathy

To build resilience we can practice self-empathy and self-compassion on a daily basis. Here are some steps to help guide you:

1. Begin to notice any negative self-talk or self-criticism—it can be for the smallest mistake that you made. Become aware of your inner dialogue.

2. For one week, keep a tally of how many times and in what situations you did this.

3. In the next week, catch yourself being critical of yourself and replace that thought with a kind or compassionate thought. Forgive yourself for the mistake and talk to yourself like you would your best friend. What do you tell your friends when they fail? Treat yourself like you would your best friend. Notice what begins to shift and journal what you discover.

4. Continue this practice until those negative thoughts get quieter, until they become merely a whisper. This might take a few weeks, or it might take a few months, but you will notice a shift. Take some time to journal about how this has impacted how you show up, how you handle feedback, and how you lead others.

The Power of Empathy

When I heard Joan Blades, founder of MoveOn.org, speak at The Global Women's Summit in San Francisco, I was expecting to find a pretty tough, strong, and outspoken woman who was angry at the injustices of the world and was fighting for our democracy. To my surprise, she was nothing like that. She was small in her physique, with a soft-spoken voice and a very nurturing and feminine energy about her. She sat up on stage with a few other equally powerful women and started talking about her work as an activist and a change maker. I didn't sense any anger coming from her whatsoever, no resentment, blame, or finger pointing. Instead, what I felt was an immense earnestness and caring about the state of our democracy that was palpable; she had a real desire to understand why things were the way they were and to find pathways towards change. What struck me the most was her current work of uniting the deep divide between the Republican and Democratic sides of our democracy.

She spoke about her desire to really understand the psychology of Republicans, really understand their needs, values, and goals. A staunch liberal herself, I was wondering why on earth she thought this might be even remotely possible—unite the division in our democracy that was now completely dysfunctional? That's a big issue to tackle! But tackle she did, by coming up with an initiative called Living Room Conversations. This is an opportunity for Democrats and Liberals to invite their Republican friends over to their house to have a candid conversation about their beliefs and values to look for commonality and build connection.

According to their website, one of the successes of this approach was a high-profile conversation on crony capitalism, co-hosted by Mark Meckler of Tea Party Patriots and Joan Blades, where they identified the need for criminal justice reform as one of a number of areas of solid common ground for further discussion and future collaborative action, which is a topic now being addressed in Congress. Other organizations are adopting the format and applying it to address critical issues in their communities, and it is serving as a framework that can help bring people together to transform not just the political system, but many facets of civil society.

For me, this is a great example of empathic leadership in action. Through her visionary leadership, Joan is showing us that when we sit down and just listen to the other side, even when there is deep division between two parties (as well as anger, fear, and resentment), it is possible to work through the differences and find commonality from which to work. Living Room Conversations is an embodiment of empathic communication at its finest—refraining from blame or pointing fingers, listening deeply, putting yourself in the other's shoes, and understanding how they feel and what they value.

Through this practice, important steps are being taken to reshape our communities and political system. This type of deep dialogue in all areas of our economic and societal structures is essential if we are to be able to find a way forward. Joan Blade's incredible leadership is not only inspiring but is a reminder of what is possible when women lean into their natural gift of empathic communication and bring it forth to use in a positive way for change.

The Use of Dialogue To Tackle Gender Bias

One of the most powerful tools we have to tackle issues such as gender bias is similar to what Joan Blades is using to unite Republicans and Democrats. Deep dialogue among people with differing worldviews is hugely under-utilized in organizations because we don't have a precedent for it. We rarely invite the other side to sit down to openly express their views without judgment—even the ones that might not be "PC" or "acceptable" in a corporate or business setting. Instead we spend millions of dollars on "diversity agendas" or training that doesn't really move the needle toward our desired goals of more understanding, inclusion, and equality. Perhaps adopting this structure of open dialogue could be the next step in tackling the gender issue and in overcoming the deep biases that restrain the forward movement of women in leadership.

The first step where deep dialogue could be used is with groups of women in conversation with each other. There are so many issues that women are up against, from how to juggle work and life balance, to how to overcome gender stereotypes or how to address the generational gap. Giving women the platform to openly discuss these issues with one another can be amazingly healing, transformative, and game changing. Many organizations have women's networks or communities that specialize in bringing together women from different levels in the organization, and this could be a great arena for hosting conversations about these types of topics as well.

For those who think including men in the discussion is a better way to go, I wholeheartedly agree. I believe that in order to tackle the gender-gap issues that exist today, we need to extend a hand to men and invite them into the conversation so they can be vocal advocates on our behalf. It's also important for us to talk to them in a safe and open space about the biases and stereotypes that keep women from advancing in leadership, without worrying about being politically correct. And while we're at it, how about if we talk about how we can transform our organizations from the inside out to create places where people can truly thrive and prosper, workplaces which are more sustainable and designed for humans, not just for generating money!

These are just a few of the issues that we can tackle if we create the opportunities for dialogue. I've personally been a part of helping large companies create and foster inclusive cultures through dialogue as part of larger culture change initiatives initiated by their top leaders. It is encouraging and hopefully can also act as examples for other organizations to do the same. But if our leaders don't see the value it is up to all of us to feel empowered enough to point out the need to have those conversations. As women leaders, I do believe we have to speak up and say something if we want anything to change. However, I personally believe that women must have the opportunity to have these conversations amongst themselves, before inviting men into the discussion. Once we can truly stand in our Empowered Feminine and lead from a place of empathy and compassion instead of from blame and judgment, will men want to listen and engage in conversation with us. Unfortunately, there are still too many angry feminists out there that actively work to alienate the few men that are willing to help us. To those women I say: heal your anger and stop sabotaging women's advancement! To women who have been victims of this or other types of sabotage by women, I say practice forgiveness and letting go. Easier said than done, but a very important piece if we want to invite men in constructive and collaborative dialogue.

Let's Talk About Men

Since we're talking about empathy and tackling gender bias, let's talk about the elephant in the room: men. It goes without saying that men play an integral role in women's advancement, and we need them as allies, advocates, and partners if we want to see transformative change. They are in decision-making positions and have the power to prioritize diversity and gender equality in organizations. We must engage with them if we are to move past gender bias, sexism, and discrimination. To achieve that goal, we need to practice empathy.

Let's start with going back into time and looking at the beginnings of the feminist movement. If we want to understand men, we can't do that without examining how this huge social movement impacted men. After centuries and eons of servitude, women suddenly had a voice. They were liberating themselves, leaving the household to realize their full potential, and were demanding equal rights. And to top it all off, they were entering the workforce in droves, taking away jobs once held by men. Not only were women competent, they seemed to be able to be good at all sorts of things, from multi-tasking to negotiation. Is it any wonder that this might have left men feeling threatened? Their very existence was being challenged! As women gained more and more power, taking over the roles traditionally held by men only, the very notion of masculinity was under attack.

If we are to heal the wounding of centuries of persecution, we must first explore men's psyche to understand how women's empowerment has affected them and to realize the unintentional negative impact it has had on our ability to work collaboratively with them. Since we're talking about empathy, women might start practicing it to understand what men as a whole might have been going through as women liberated themselves and began demanding equal rights.

One of the ways in which people protect themselves when they feel attacked or threatened in any way is to blame, victimize, and feel better-than. They tend to only see the flaws in others. And this is what leads to micro-inequities, where we subconsciously choose to treat people in a way that makes them feel disrespected, blamed, or as an object. This can often lead to conflict and tension, leading to a breakdown in communication, ultimately harming the relationship.

One of the subtle (and sometimes not-so-subtle) effects of women liberating themselves has been the subsequent victimization of women by men. A theory that I have about this is that this was done (and still continues) not in a conscious attempt to hurt women, but a subconscious attempt by men to hold on to their power and influence in the world, as a means of self-protection and self-preservation. By going into their better-than place, men have protected their sense of self, their very identity. The threat that women have posed for so very long has led men and our entire society to objectify women, leading to the notion that women are inferior and incapable. When we put ourselves in men's shoes it becomes easier to understand how feeling threatened by women's power would prompt oppressive behavior, which has continued straight into the workplace, as we see with sexism and harassment.

This is by no means a justification of men's behavior or a way to dismiss the harmful and damaging consequences this has had and continues to have on women's self-image and self-worth and on our efforts to become equals. It is however, the first step into acceptance and understanding, eventually leading us down the path of forgiveness. Without it we will continue to perpetuate the cycle of victimization, internalizing the attacks, buying into the cultural stereotypes and messages that are aimed at keeping women away from realizing and stepping into their real power. The anger and blame that women hold has grown over decades (if not eons) of oppression, and it won't just magically disappear. Instead it will foster the ill treatment of men, even those who are advocates of women, which will perpetuate the continued victimization of women.

Forgiveness and acceptance are the first steps toward healing that wounding and owning our true power.

By owning our power and standing in our truth from a centered and grounded place, women can request the need for dialogue on this issue. However, if we go in with a sense of victimhood, needing to prove our worth, and standing in our own better-than place, it will surely lead to a dead-end result. Skilled facilitation as well as practicing empathy, a willingness to listen deeply, withholding judgment, and telling the truth are integral for both parties to make progress in understanding each other's perspective. This will ultimately lead to collaborative solutions that can be implemented within the organization, bringing real change toward tackling bias.

Facilitating Deep Dialogue

There are some wonderful tools to facilitate deep dialogue for groups of multiple stakeholders with different worldviews, which can lead to transformation within a system that senses the need to change and is willing to put in the effort. I would not recommend people from the inside of an organization to facilitate these conversations without the leadership and guidance of a skilled practitioner. Conflict of interest, subjective bias, and lack of experience can quickly turn a good intention into a failed attempt that could do more harm than good. Having seen first-hand the power of this work, I can truly say it is one of the best and most effective approaches available to teams and organizations looking to tackle tough issues to create lasting and deep culture change. This in itself is an inherently feminine approach to driving solutions— instead of being prescriptive and pointing fingers of how people should change, we can allow all stakeholders to partake in the discussion and collectively design change.

And if the conversations aren't happening in your organizations, then I invite you to stand in your Feminine Leadership and create the opportunities. The great thing about this is that you don't have to wait around for someone else to do something about a topic you feel passionate about. This can be an empowering and effective way for anyone to tackle these issues, and begin having the conversations that truly matter, inside an organization or externally. All it really takes is having a vision, stepping into your leadership and being willing to collaborate with others who share your passion to make a difference.

Leading Gracefully

CHAPTER 9
Collaboration

The Future of Work

So far, all the leadership strengths and traits we've talked about are qualities that lead us to work in a collaborative way. The reason collaboration is so important to women and men is because the way we work is essentially shifting. We see that in subtle ways and other times in not so subtle ways. Companies are investing in people development, realizing that it is the best resource they have to stay ahead of the curve. Those who want a competitive advantage intuitively understand innovation and creativity are essential to meeting market demands and crucial in facing our collective sustainability challenges. The future of work as we know it is shifting from an outdated *directive* approach toward *collaborative* frameworks that inspire us to engage in new and different ways with our work and with each other. And that is why collaboration is the next strength featured in the FLM.

Fostering Collaboration in Organizations

Many great companies that operate today still work in a hierarchical system, plagued by red tape, bureaucracy and politics. In one of the diversity and inclusion sessions I led recently, employees openly admitted that they were more competitive with one another than with their actual external competitors. This sort of in-fighting only limits the organization's effectiveness, productivity and ultimately its ability to meet customer needs and demands. It also limits innovation and the ability to come up with the next great idea. But we see it time and time again, especially in larger, traditional companies that are stuck in the old paradigm. It's reflected in the structure, but also in the organizational culture. People feel afraid to speak up, they conform to cultural norms and "play the game" in order to get ahead. All this greatly stifles the ability to collaborate and work well amongst teams and departments and is one of the biggest challenges companies face today. Luckily, the tide is turning with companies like Facebook, Twitter and Airbnb who make it a point to create cultures where collaboration and innovation can thrive. But it can still be a challenge to make sure we are inclusive leaders, making sure everyone's voice is heard and working in a way that we can get the best from our people resources.

As leaders, we all have a responsibility to take a step back and assess how collaborative our teams are, and if there is any room for improvement. It's difficult to do this given all the myriad issues and challenges we face on a daily basis, but it is integral if you want to drive business results, better team performance, employee engagement and great ideas. So to help with that, I've created a quick test you can take to determine how collaborative you or your teams are and where you can improve.

Collaboration Litmus Test

Take a moment to reflect on you or your team's performance and engagement level. Think about how your employees work together as a team, and how well they work together crossfunctionally with other teams and departments. If you don't manage a team, you can slightly modify these questions and think about yourself as an individual, to assess how collaborative you are in your business.

1. Does my team work in a collaborative way with each other or is there competition amongst the team or with other teams? **Yes/No**

2. Are my team's efforts streamlined or is there any redundancy or double effort in work by members of my team or amongst teams? **Yes/No**

3. Are we openly sharing best practices with one another? **Yes/No**

4. Do we have regular brainstorming sessions as a team to overcome complex challenges? **Yes/No**

5. Do we have regular update meetings as a team to communicate our progress? **Yes/No**

6. Do we work well with external teams, communicating with them, asking for help and/or sharing information? **Yes/No**

7. Are my team's actions strategically aligned with business objectives or do they "act for the sake of action" because output is rewarded? **Yes/No**

8. Are all voices heard and included in the decision making process? **Yes/No**

9. Do you feel a high level of engagement and motivation on your team? **Yes/No**

10. Does my team produce innovative ideas, new ways of thinking or doing things that results in better products or service? **Yes/No**

If you answered mostly **Yes** to the questions above, then congratulations, you or your team are highly collaborative. If you answered mostly **No**, then you have a bit of work to do to achieve more collaboration. As an individual or entrepreneur, you might want to consider how collaboration could serve you, what opportunities might be possible or what it could add to your business or project. If you are a manager, think about what types of results you could achieve with your team if you were able to create a more collaborative environment. Jot down those thoughts and then make a plan, committing to actions you can take to open yourself up to more collaboration or to inspire collaboration on your teams.

How To Be a Collaborative Leader

Now that you have a pretty good idea where you land on the collaboration scale, I'm going to offer insights on some of the most important ways we can inspire collaboration on our teams. Many of these concepts have already been presented throughout the book, but I wanted to point out a few leadership qualities that are absolutely essential for collaboration. I'd like to also share some stories of cross-collaboration that might inspire you as to what is possible when we think and act in this way.

Decision by Consensus

As I briefly mentioned before, I had the opportunity to explore and experience my own collaborative leadership when co-designing and hosting the Women and Power Leadership Forum. This was an idea that emerged from my desire to facilitate a conversation about how women can redefine power and use their feminine strengths to lead in a new way. We created the conference using collaborative processes where participants collectively formed the agenda and topic items for parts of the conference. Together with the work of a wonderful team, this experience provided rich learning for all of us in exploring what it means to be collaborative.

One of the big beliefs I had about collaborative work was that one must come to decisions by consensus; if there were any outliers, you could not forge ahead. This seemed an exhaustive and almost impossible task when you think about how hard it is to get a group of people to agree on anything (especially women!). To my relief, I discovered that making the final decision wasn't as crucial as was the *process* of making the decision. Team members must have a chance to voice their opinion through open and honest dialogue, and everyone must have an opportunity to explore the issue together. This process is integral to collaborative decision-making (even though that term seems like an oxymoron!). Once you've gone through this exercise, team members usually feel comfortable with someone taking the reins and making a decision. Usually themes and patterns emerge, and the solution or decision becomes obvious. Although it can be difficult to make everyone happy, people feel good knowing their ideas were heard, even if they weren't incorporated into the final decision. Not surprisingly, the collective decision is usually a better solution or idea than what one person alone could have come up with.

The trick here is to be inclusive. We cannot achieve true collaboration unless we are including everyone's opinions and ideas. While this might sound cumbersome and time consuming, it's part of the reality of collaboration. One thing we need to consider is that sometimes we unintentionally exclude others, mainly because of our unconscious biases that lead us to gravitate towards people who are more like us, according to recent neuroscience on this subject. For instance, how many of you are introverted or have been on a team with introverts? What are your beliefs about them? What do you do to ensure that their ideas are included and heard? There is a great Ted talk by Susan Cain on the power of introverts, and in this talk she states that 50% of the population are introverted, yet we as a society tend to reward extroverts and believe they are better leaders, more confident, and have better ideas. We point the finger at introverts, thinking they are the ones that need to change and develop better communication skills or leadership skills. What we end up missing out on are all the great, well thought out ideas they have to offer. Because introverts do just that—they take more time to think through problems, but often come up with better ideas than extroverts who tend to think off the cuff. This is just to exemplify how we as leaders need to do more to become aware of our biases to make sure we are including everyone, and not missing out on great talent that is staring us in the face.

Leaning In vs. Leaning Out

The other assumption I was holding about collaboration was that having a vision and inspiring people to join you was enough to be collaborative. I thought that using collaborative words like "our" or "together" inspired a sense of "we are all in this together." Wrong. Turns out words aren't enough. As leaders, we assume that leading means doing it all. For many of us, the fear of failing, embarrassment, or being seen as weak have us hanging on to control. We take on more than we should, we step on toes, and we micro-manage without meaning to. Not surprisingly, the signal that you send by doing this is that "she's got it covered." As I mentioned in earlier chapters, women tend to do this to a fault—we take on more than we can chew because we are good multi-taskers and want to prove our value, and in doing so, prevent others from stepping in. This is where the now proverbial "leaning in" approach is NOT effective. By "leaning out" as leaders, we give our people a chance to lean in. This creates an opportunity for them to take responsibility for the tasks at hand, to step in and contribute more fully and engages them in a way where their best ideas and input are brought forth. This can be one of the biggest challenges to overcome. Learning to let go and trust others is crucial to create the space for brilliance to shine. Finding the balance is where this practice becomes an art form.

Vulnerability as Strength

I've talked about vulnerability earlier, but I truly believe it is the single most important key to success in any collaborative process. We've got it all wrong in our work ethos. We believe vulnerability is a weakness. We are afraid to admit we don't have the answer for fear of being seen as incompetent. Our need to prove our worth and value and the fear of shame all lead to creating separation. What I have found over and over again in my own leadership journey is that when I am willing to be vulnerable, when I am able to listen to feedback and be willing to receive it fully without taking it personally, these acts are powerful beyond measure. This is a secret superpower that everyone possesses, but not everyone has the courage to enact. It takes a willingness to fail and learn from your mistakes and to risk the shame that comes along with it. But the rewards are bountiful. It's the quickest route to creating trust in any relationship or group process. It creates an environment where others feel able to open up and share their feelings, stimulating input, ideas, and solutions. It allows us to be human, and realize that we are all in this together. It opens up our hearts and reminds us that it's not always about the bottom line, or even the next big idea. It's about building relationships with others and creating great ideas together, which makes the work that much more rewarding and innovative.

I'm grateful for the opportunity to have worked with women who had the capacity to support me and give me feedback. Learning to give credit and acknowledging your partners and teammates goes without saying, yet how many times do we just breeze over that part? Being vulnerable, setting your ego aside, and letting go of the need to shine are unique aspects of collaborative leadership which are hard to learn and hard to teach. For many of us, this is counter-intuitive to the competitive nature of business. But it's an integral part of how we operate as human beings, and it's the missing key that leads to collective success. Think about what might be different if you adopted this mind-set in the way you manage your teams. What would need to change or shift in yourself to allow for more collaborative thinking and action to come forward in how you manage your team or business? What might be the positive or negative outcomes from that action?

Being Daring

Taking risks is another thing men do well, and is the reason why we classify it as a masculine strength. It's part of the FLM because being daring separates good leaders from great leaders. At a time where our planet faces so many challenges, thinking outside the box and taking risks is essential to developing the necessary technologies and innovations needed to be able to face those challenges. However, many women still tend to play it safe by playing small. Afraid to take risks for fear of failure or being seen as too "opinionated," we hold ourselves back. Thinking of the long-term impacts of our decisions is maybe part of the reason we tend to be more conservative in our approach, and I would say that is a good thing. But where it becomes an impediment is when we don't lean in or participate because of fear or negative self-talk that limits our expression. We can learn how to be more daring by giving up our fear of shame and embracing our vulnerability. No one likes to make a mistake or say the wrong thing or make the wrong decision. But "fail fast, fail often" as Steve Jobs once said is what leads to great ideas, amazing inventions like the iPhone, or the light bulb for that matter. In fact, Edison went through 10,000 prototypes before he was able to successfully invent the light bulb. About all his failed attempts, he said, "I have not failed 10,000 times. I have not failed once. I have succeeded in proving that those 10,000 ways will not work. When I have eliminated the ways that will not work, I will find the way that will work." Imagine what our world would be like if he gave up on the 9,999th time?

When we dare greatly and let go of our need to fit in or be accepted by others, we are more likely to take risks, think outside the box and try new things. Of course, everything needs to be done with thought, and we should make sure we're not taking risks that can cause undue harm. But as a whole, I think women can afford to take more risks, whether it's in the boardroom or in our lives and businesses.

Encouragingly, as I write this, I see more and more women speaking up and challenging the status quo. From demanding equal pay or speaking out about the blatant sexism that exists in many industries like Hollywood, women are daring to do something about the issues that affect all of us. You might call it the next wave of feminism, but what is obvious is that if women don't call out the injustices in the world, the powers that be will continue trying to take away our hard won rights. The same applies to the corporate world. There are decisions that are being made in companies worldwide that we all know aren't in the interest of our communities or our planet. If you are a woman executive who has influence, why not speak up and say something if you're conscious is telling you to do so?

Think about it—what would happen if all women in the United States stood up and demanded six months paid maternity leave? Or what if all women in the Muslim world stood up and demanded to join the rest of the world in terms of women's rights? What would happen is what has happened throughout history—collective activism leading to collective change. The same goes for changing the masculine and feminine balance in the corporate world. When more and more women dare to embody Feminine Leadership, we will reach a critical mass where this then becomes the norm for both men and women. In order to shift the masculine paradigm where risks are taken just for short-term profit or to benefit a few people, we can begin to see that taking risks in the feminine paradigm is about social change, creating balance and doing what is right for the collective. Finding our tribe and collaborating with like-minded people will help us achieve those goals, but we must first take a bold step toward action.

The Outcome

The proof is in the pudding they say. You might be wondering how this collaborative process to produce the women's conference worked out for me in the end. I'm happy to say that we successfully co-created a first-time event, which was sold out and created a buzz in Silicon Valley. As hosts, we put these collaborative principles into practice and co-led a day of deep dialogue for multi-generational women leaders who came together to discuss the future of power and leadership for women. We weren't attached to any outcomes and stood firmly in our vision and desire to create a space for women to explore the meaning of feminine leadership. Many women took away tangible resources to help them move forward in their own lives. They all learnt ways to redefine success and power structures and to create a more sustainable future for both men and women. And best of all, many wonderful partnerships and relationships arose out of that day, leading to powerful actions that have had their own ripple effects. To find out more, you can visit: www.womenandpowerforum.com

Cross-Sector Collaboration—A New Frontier

As we progress into the 21st century, we are beginning to move away from directive frameworks. Stepping away from the top-down, silo'd structures that have kept us locked into separateness and away from this notion of interdependence and inter-connectedness, we begin to move toward systems that are more flat, networked, and interlaced. The best example we have of this is the Internet. The World Wide Web—a kaleidoscope of information and knowledge that can teach us virtually anything we want to learn, as well as social media which has connected the globe and enabled social and political movements. Yet we are still stuck in the old paradigm, in a system that keeps us separate. From our organizational systems to our political systems, we still operate in silos. Isn't it time we catch up with the times we live in?

Cross-sector collaboration—the synergy of different areas of knowledge and expertise coming together to solve a shared problem, is where our society is aching to go. We see now that working in silos or acting alone cannot solve the complexity of the issues that we are faced with. We must break free of this model of thinking and enter into a new mode, one that is inherently more feminine in nature. If we were to apply feminine concepts to how we tackle global issues, what would be different? How would we operate? What if, for a moment, we dared to think outside of the box? What might be possible? And in our organizations, what would be possible if there was more collaboration between teams, departments, leaders and industries?

Cross-Sector Collaboration in Virology

A great example of Feminine Leadership at play with a cross-sector collaborative approach is the story of Ilaria Capua, an Italian virologist who was working on the H7N1 virus, better known as avian flu. This virus causes immense suffering to animals, can lead to death within 48 hours (in animals), and can also spread into humans. In 2000, Ilaria was faced with managing one of the biggest outbreaks of avian influenza that had ever occurred. This flu spread from Asia into Central Europe, and then into Africa, destroying the poultry industry everywhere it hit. There was no prior experience in how to manage this type of outbreak, and it ended up killing 17 million birds before it was eradicated.

Luckily, Ilaria and her team were able to isolate the genetic sequence for avian flu. Unfortunately, there was no information about the virus in the genetic database, and it was impossible to share genetic sequencing data they had discovered with the wider scientific community to work on a cure collectively. In fact, after the discovery of the strain, she received a call from the World Health Organization, which asked her for the viral sequence so they could put it into a "password-protected database" which would make her "part of the club." According to Ilaria, the fear around data sharing was due to the existing dogma that stated, "scientists are too busy to share" and "scientists are going to steal the data from each other."

She was also told that it was impossible to vaccinate against avian flu, eradicate it, and still maintain exports. She knew that this had been done successfully for other animal diseases, so she and her team went on to develop the "DIVA" (Differentiating Infected from Vaccinated Animals) vaccination strategy, which led to the eradication of the virus and since 2005, has been included as protocol for animal flu outbreaks.

Capua risked her reputation and said no to the WHO because she believed that in order to make faster progress, the international community should have access to the virus so that everyone could work on it, especially on a virus that had the potential to become a pandemic. In fact, after they finally published the sequence, it was subsequently downloaded 1000 times in one week. Through advocating for more transparency and sharing of scientific data, Ilaria received a lot of support from people who were managing the crisis, as well as a lot of criticism and backlash.

In the end, the international debate that evolved led to a new paradigm which convinced scientists worldwide to support data sharing, something that had never had a precedent in this field. It also lead to the resolution put out by the OIE (World Organization for Animal Health), that any lab which receives samples for avian flu *had* to deposit them in a public database within three months for accessibility by the larger scientific community. And in 2011, the WHO passed a resolution as a landmark agreement that *all* influenza samples will be shared with partners who need them to support public health, which came through the efforts of Ilaria and the veterinary world, which has fundamentally changed how the world shares data about influenza.

For Capua, it was unimaginable that scientists should work in silos. "I personally believe that when it comes to public health issues, you can't keep your information sitting in a drawer because you think you have to wait until someone publishes it." Yet this was how the old system worked. Capua's vision sounds logical—why wouldn't we want a new model that could bring forward innovative solutions much faster and cut down on both human and animal suffering and loss? Yet changing the old system wasn't as easy as she had imagined. She had to risk her career to fight for her vision. But today, because of her leadership, she has established the "One Flu for One Health" initiative to foster interdisciplinary collaboration and transparency between vets and medical scientists, developing a sharing platform which is setting a standard for the entire scientific community and helping combat the looming threat of a future pandemic.

Ilaria's story is only one among many others, but it shows that a fundamental shift begins in the way we think. As leaders we must think more broadly and be willing to let go of dogma, and realize that multi-disciplinary approaches are the way of the future. Doing things for personal fame or gain cannot serve the greater good. Holding on to ideas or acting alone doesn't lead to breakthroughs in science, technology, and the like. From the open-source movement, to widely distributed content, to global educational platforms, the wave has already begun. We must continue to look at things from a broader perspective if we are to appropriately tackle the challenges of tomorrow. As we saw with Ilaria's example, women can be the trailblazers and visionaries to lead systems and organizations, to foster cross-sector collaboration, and to build strategic partnerships and community while staying true to their values.

Leading Gracefully

CHAPTER 10
Humility

Check Your Ego at the Door and People Will Follow

So how do we become true collaborative leaders? Humility is the next strength featured in the FLM and is one of the most significant ways we can get there. To do this, we need to let go of our ego and constantly remind ourselves that we don't necessarily have all the answers. This can be especially hard for women who are constantly trying to prove their self-worth and value. As we step more powerfully into our leadership, the temptation to be "leader-like" through adopting a traditional perspective of leadership, (i.e., using a more directive, top-down leadership style), will always be there. This more masculine approach is fine and sometimes can be useful in certain situations. But if our aim is to inspire collaboration and innovation, we need a different approach. We need to check our egos at the door.

If we look to the other side of the spectrum, if we stand in the Disempowered Feminine, the risk could be that we become too humble. Many women don't like to boast about their achievements. We also tend to be more introverted, fly under the radar, work tirelessly, and do a great job, yet sometimes we don't get the credit when it is deserved. We can also be too shy to advocate for ourselves or our team's efforts, which then go unnoticed. To add insult to injury, because women have a hard time saying no or asking for help, they'll just tend to take on more and more work. Over time, these women either get burned out or get resentful, which doesn't help career advancement or job fulfillment and just isn't sustainable.

The other approach is to fully stand in the Empowered Feminine. This is where we own our achievements and those of others and happily give other's due credit, while being able to share our own achievements when necessary. By taking a feminine approach, we let go of the need to have all the answers, and allow for the answers to emerge from mysterious places. Perhaps it's through asking your team to brainstorm possibilities or asking peers for their opinions, but by being open to new and different ideas, we allow the brilliance of others to shine, instead of having to do it all ourselves and take all the glory.

How Humble Are You?

Exercise #14

Before moving forward, it might be helpful to assess where you fall on the spectrum of humility. Take this quick exercise to determine where you land.

1. On a scale of 1 to 10, what would you rate yourself in terms of how humble are you in a work environment?

2. What is the impact of that (positive or negative)?

3. How much visibility do you have across your organization?

4. How often do you give credit to others for your achievements?

5. Do your superiors take all the credit for your work?

6. In order to be more effective, do you need to practice more humility or less?

7. What steps can you take to be more balanced as it relates to humility?

This exercise should give you a perspective on how humble you are and what areas you need to work on to have more balance. Going back to the 4 Quadrants, think about your desired impact. Which qualities might you need to pull in to create more balance and have a more integrated approach? What would change for you in your leadership style if you adopted those behaviors?

Learning To Be Humble

I first met Julie at a woman's empowerment event in Los Angeles, where she was a featured panelist speaking about her experience starting a tech company. She spoke openly and honestly about her journey going from a very successful media executive to a first-time tech entrepreneur. Her business idea came from many years of running vision-board workshops for women whom she referred to as her "Bettys." Because these experiences had been so powerful in helping women catalyze and manifest their deep desires, she, along with her business partner Lindsey Heisser, wanted to bring that same experience to a wider audience. So they decided to build an online visioning tool, which they named Bettyvision. They successfully rose seed funding from friends and family to fund the development of the platform, and went into beta testing. Through this feedback, they found out that in order to make their digital tool effective, they were going to have to make some changes, which was going to take more money. On top of that, they experienced a few legal hurdles as they went through the tech development phase, due to blunders that many first-time entrepreneurs make.

Julie found herself working in the trenches of Bettyvision's tech development. These day-to-day tasks were far from her passion of helping people realize their dreams and goals. As they continued to tweak the tool and went to look for a second round of funding, it was clear that the hurdles were too high, and the money wasn't easy to find. However, there was a light at the end of the tunnel—Bettyvision was a big hit with Millennials who liked the idea of focusing on their career goals and aligning their personal and professional values with the organizations they worked for.

It was at this point that Julie and Lindsey decided to pivot— instead of giving up, and instead of forging down the path *they* thought was best, they humbly listened to customer feedback. They realized that the tool they had developed could be more useful in helping organizations with their visioning strategy, rather than individual women, which would make it a big value-add for companies. And that's when Tribemint was born—a branding and creative marketing agency dedicated to helping companies connect with Millennials through inspired vision, culture, and engagement. Since then, Julie and Lindsey have had non-stop conversations with clients eager to engage in visioning work to create campaigns that will help reach a younger market.

When asking Julie how she feels about it—she says she has no regrets and doesn't see Bettyvision as a failure, or that she gave up on her original vision to help empower women. "Our company will still be focused on women as an important sector, and we will still cater to that niche as we grow and expand in other ways to help fund and mentor women in tech. We want to help women accelerate in their goals to be entrepreneurs and avoid some of the pitfalls we experienced. It really requires a certain type of humbleness and vulnerability to accept your failures and move past them quickly—and it's something women have to get better at mastering."

Julie and Lindsey's stories are a great example of how women can learn from their failures, instead of viewing them as roadblocks. Because they were able to humbly accept what customers were saying about Bettyvision, they quickly realized that they had to pivot and try something new. They didn't take it personally, and they didn't give up. They continued to listen to feedback and take advice, while staying in alignment with their own values. Once they found that sweet spot, they were able to quickly move forward with a new concept that worked better. Instead of letting failure stop them, they accepted the facts and turned the learning into a much more successful venture for themselves and their customers.

Staying Open to Possibility

Is it hard to swallow our pride and admit that something isn't working? Of course it is! But it is our attachments to the expected outcome that create those disappointments. When we stay unattached, we stay much more open to what the Universe or life has to offer. As leaders in a business setting, we often feel like we have to have all the answers and great ideas. But often the best ideas get generated from the collective wisdom of the team, not from just one individual. Learning to let go of our ego, and the need to be in the spotlight, or to receive all the credit, we can then create an atmosphere that encourages others to participate fully.

This more feminine approach to 'doing' requires staying present to our 'being.' By being present to what wants to emerge instead of always directing, we become more tuned into our surroundings, tuned into our customer's feedback, and to the needs of the market or other stakeholders. We invite others to join the process of creating which not only stimulates engagement but also gives people purpose and meaning. This is what true Feminine Leadership is all about. By making space and including ideas and input, instead of doing it all ourselves we head toward more innovation and the ability to adapt and pivot more quickly—an essential skill set for any team, business, or organization in the 21st century.

Gaining Visibility and Ending the Bullying

Another piece of the humble pie is learning how to walk the tightrope as it relates to gaining visibility, first for ourselves and then for the people who work for us. Gaining visibility is important for upward mobility and career growth, and, ladies, that means building relationships outside of your department or immediate area of responsibility. It also means making sure you gain valuable face time with key decision makers.

For example, a senior woman at Cisco gains visibility by reaching out and scheduling lunches with VPs in departments that she might be interested in working with one day. Another senior female manager volunteers to plan social and fundraising activities within the company. Small actions like that might be time-consuming, but they can greatly benefit your opportunities when the time comes for advancement. One client of mine, a VP of Finance, decided that the best way to gain visibility for her and her team was to give regular updates during global finance conference calls, which she would typically stay quiet on. That one action helped her gain much-deserved recognition and set her up for the promotion she wanted. The same goes for women who are running businesses—taking the time to build visibility in your sector is key.

The risk of not doing this cannot only be detrimental to how others perceive you, but it can have harmful effects on your career and the careers of the women who work for you. For women who are just starting out, it can be difficult to get the recognition or credit they deserve unless their managers make sure to advocate on their behalf. I've heard too many stories of senior women managers taking all the credit for the hard work of their younger associates. This can shatter self-confidence and create major resentment, and it might be a reason women opt out.

In fact, research has identified that one of the main reasons women opt out in mid-career is not because they want to leave and start families, but because of a lack of role models, mentoring, and problems with supervisory relationships. According to a study by the Center for Work-Life Policy, 74% of women in technology reported "loving their work," yet these women left their careers at a staggering rate. 56% of technical women leave at the mid-level point, just when the loss of their talent is most costly to companies. This is more than double the quit rate for men. It is also higher than the quit rate for women in science and engineering.

Let's take a moment and acknowledge that micro-managing, bullying, and other mean-spirited competitive behavior among women is unfortunately alive and well and adds to the already tough challenges women face as they look to build their careers. I don't want to point fingers or to generalize, but it's something women have to face in themselves. Instead of taking all the glory, we need to give credit where credit is due. If you feel threatened by your female employee or colleague, ask yourself why do you feel threatened? How can you leverage her strengths to benefit the team and larger organization instead of putting her down or trying to outshine her? If you recognize this behavior in yourself, you might want to ask yourself—what is it that creates the need to act this way? Which traits from the FLM do you need more of to balance your leadership style so that you can become more inclusive? These are very important questions for all women to ask themselves so that we can begin to build supportive networks where women help each other succeed and get to the next level, instead of competing with one another and holding one another back, adding to the gender gap problem that currently exists.

Creating an Inclusive Climate

Another reason why women tend to opt-out is because of un-conscious biases. The greatest leaders know that to get the best from people means creating an atmosphere where people can thrive. The way to achieve this is through creating inclusive cultures where differences, whether they are gender, communi-cation style, personality, cultural background, race, sexuality, or appearance, are all treated equally. Our hidden beliefs are what drive our actions and behaviors, so the more aware of our bi-ases we become, the more we can choose a different belief that serves our goal of inclusion.

I'd like to share an example of the importance of inclusion in a story of an organization where I work as an executive coach. This international company has a holding in one of the post-Soviet Union countries, and at one point this site was hav-ing major problems with decreasing production levels and de-creasing profit year over year. After some time, the corporate executives decided to send in a team of ex-pats to "save the day" and fix issues plaguing this site. They came in with new and innovative solutions and began to implement them right away, without including any of the local management team in those decisions. Unfortunately, their behavior caused this team to lose trust in the ex-pats, whom they viewed as outsiders who did not respect them or their knowledge. Communica-tion began to breakdown and after six months, nothing was accomplished. Huge rifts were created and the ex-pats ended up leaving, and they were back at square one.

This story is a great example of the significance of inclusive leadership and cultures, and how even big international com-panies sometimes forget the importance of this behavior. I often wonder what would have been different if the ex-pats sat down with the local team, got their input, and collaborated to find the best solutions instead of disregarding their ideas and expertise. In the end, we can have all sorts of diversity, but if we don't take time to leverage that diversity, it can backfire and lead to less than desired business results.

We all have biases that live in our subconscious that are quietly running the show. They are telling us who we should and shouldn't like, who to hire and who to promote, and even who we should trust. Our unconscious beliefs lead us to act in certain ways that signal to others how we really feel about them, called "micro-inequities." Over time, if people sense that they aren't being included, appreciated, or liked by their peers, they mentally check out and sometimes eventually leave the organization. This can have significant consequences on motivation level, performance, trust, and ultimately on how the team and organization operate. As leaders we need to have self-awareness and make sure we are being inclusive instead of unintentionally putting people at a disadvantage through our unconscious behaviors.

Asking for input and feedback from others, making sure people's opinions are heard, and giving a chance for them to truly express themselves goes a long way in creating collab- orative environments. As women, we can sometimes neglect to do this, mainly because we want to be viewed as intelligent and "in charge" by having all the answers. But we all know that leads to feeling overwhelmed, and ultimately does a big disservice to those on your team because it takes away the op- portunity for others to learn and contribute. If we can let go of the need to be perceived as "the expert" and establish trust with our people, it will make it that much easier for people to follow. This creates more time for you to take on the role of a mentor/coach, helping your people develop skills, make bet- ter decisions, and troubleshoot where necessary. In essence, it makes leading a lot easier and more graceful, and much more effective!

I'll invite you for just a minute to think about some of the people you work with. What assumptions or beliefs might you be holding about them? Who do you have an affinity for? Who is in your in-group vs. your out group? How might your beliefs be affecting your working relationships? How do your past experiences affect how you view certain groups of people?

Less Judgment, More Acceptance

Let's face it, women can be judgmental, especially when it comes to other women. We can be competitive with one another, we can compare ourselves to other women, and we can be overly critical too. There is a pervasive "scarcity" mentality that women hold, believing for some reason that there are limited positions at the top and not a lot of room for many women at the table. This creates a competitive environment. All these things have led to a situation where many women simply don't support one another in the workplace as much as they could. There certainly isn't such a thing as the "girl's club"—at least to my knowledge!

We do, however, have a fair share of professional women's networks, women's initiatives, and the like. And there are some organizations that do a great job at this—like Watermark for Women based in Silicon Valley and Women in Technology International (WITI), Women 2.0, Professional Women's Network in Europe, and many others. But when it comes down to it, women have a long way to go in supporting and helping one another up the proverbial ladder. The generational gap is becoming wider and wider as Millennials begin to flood the talent pool, and they seem to have a totally different perspective on how things should be.

What tends to get in the way are the assumptions and judgments we make up about each other, leading us to treat others in a way that is less than favorable. What we need and what I've seen work beautifully, are candid conversations amongst women of different generations to discuss their differences and learn from each other's worldviews and experiences. The only way we're going to find ways to get along and be supportive of one another is by accepting each other and letting go of the baggage. When we become less judgmental, and more forgiving of women who might be slightly different than us, it can lead us to work better together and to form alliances that can give women the boost they need to face the myriad other challenges they have to deal with in the workplace.

Identifying Our Bias

Exercise #15

This exercise is to help you become more aware of your judgments and assumptions of other women, and to help you become more inclusive. I recommend choosing a woman you are in conflict with or you have a hard time getting along with. Run through the following steps and journal about your findings.

1. **Awareness:** The first step to uncover any assumptions you might be holding is by building self-awareness. Think about the women you work with—what are the stories you've made up about them? What assumptions might you be holding about them? How is this affecting how you treat them or your

relationship with them? How is it impacting your performance?

2. **Question your assumptions:** Once we're aware of our assumptions, we need to find a way to question them and find out if they are based in any fact. Ask yourself—is what I'm telling myself real or just a story I've created about this person or group of people? How is this serving me (or not serving me)? Find out if your assumptions are protecting you somehow (do you feel threatened by that person?)

3. **Choose a Different View:** If you realize that the assumptions you've got are simply not true, choose a different perspective. Find evidence or facts— take the time to really get to know the person or ask them questions and get curious. You might find out something entirely new about them or even learn a thing or two from them!

4. **Acceptance:** If that person is different than you, how might you find ways to accept them for who they are? Can you let go of any feelings that are getting in the way? What might the value of this be to your relationship? How will your team or organization benefit from this?

As we've seen, humility can be multifaceted and depending on where you fall on the humility scale, you might have different skills to develop to find the right balance. It's not always easy, and women have the added challenge of being perceived as too aggressive when advocating for themselves. But when we are able to be more inclusive, we create an atmosphere where people are motivated to do their best work, are more creative, and can feel more fulfilled. It's the most effective way to get the best out of others and create a place where people can do great work. As a leader, it will make you shine without you having to hog up the entire spotlight, and it will result in your team producing better results, including more innovation. After all, isn't that what organizations are looking for in their top talent? Here's a quick checklist so you can find the right balance with humility to help you become more effective and inclusive as a female leader:

1. **Don't control.** Allow your team members to come up with solutions and ideas instead of micro-managing or being directive.

2. **Be an advocate.** Find opportunities to gain visibility for you and your team's achievements.

3. **Visibility.** Build relationships with key stakeholders to gain more visibility across your organization or in your sector.

4. **Give credit where credit is due.** Find opportunities to openly acknowledge your team's individual and collective achievements.

5. **Give back.** Mentor and coach others, especially women who are just starting out or are more junior than you.

6. **Review your assumptions.** Take the time to reflect on the assumptions and judgments you hold about other women and shift out of those that aren't inclusive.

CHAPTER 11
Become a Game-Changer

Women Changing the World

So far we've talked a lot about women in the workplace and how we can adopt the qualities of Feminine Leadership to be more effective in business. But there might be a certain subset of women reading this book who are ready to leave the corporate world (or have already left), to start a business or create a movement of some kind to make a difference in the world. Many women are waking up to their highest potential as the world faces more and more challenges in every sector from education to politics, to the environment. As Charles Eisenstein says, "We are in the space between stories, as the old story breaks down and the new one begins to emerge." The problem is that many of us don't know what that new story is going to look like, or rather how we're going to get there. There is an urge or a hunger for us to do something more, to get into some sort of action to help change things in some small (or not so small) ways.

My intention in writing this book was to awaken the dormant power that lies in every woman. Whether you have grandiose plans and aspirations or not, every single woman on earth has the power to move mountains. I've seen it time and time again with stories of empowerment in remote regions in the world where all the odds were stacked against them. On a global scale, it seems that women are waking up to this fact and beginning to mobilize to bring about change in the respective corners of the world. But because of our privilege and advancement of the past 100 years, Western women have an advantage and therefore a bigger responsibility than other women in parts of the world that might still be struggling for basic rights and protections. As the Dali Lama stated, "The world will be saved by the Western Woman." I agree with the Dali Lama, and believe that through empowerment and getting into action, Western women will be instrumental in driving the changes needed to save the world.

Now I realize this is a tall order and a grand vision, but think about it. Do you think women who are fully empowered and balanced within the strengths and traits of the FLM would make the same decisions as their male counterparts? If women held 86% of top executive positions as men currently do, would we be putting shareholder value before those of all stakeholders (employees, the community, and the planet)? Would we be so quick to invest trillions of dollars into the military industrial complex while 16 million children live below the poverty level in this country? Would we ship our jobs to other countries because it was good for the bottom line? Or would we be so quick to make risky bets with other peoples' money, putting the entire global economy at risk?

I'm sure you would agree that the answer to all of the above questions would be NO. However, if you look at some of the women presidents in other countries, or even some of the current and former female CEOs, you wouldn't necessarily think they were any different than their male counterparts for the most part. It depends on the type of woman who is holding the position, and that's why this work is so important, especially for the next generation of women leaders. We have to make it OK and acceptable for women (and men) to embrace the power of their intuition, vulnerability, and empathy, whether it's how they make decisions, the type of businesses they run, or how they manage teams. We need more women who are courageous enough to go against the grain and show up in a different way. The world needs women (and men) who will carry out business with a balanced and feminine approach.

Creating Movements Together

For those of you who are actively engaged in social change or are thinking about starting a social movement of some kind, I say Go Girl! One of the biggest challenges women face is the tendency to think they need to do it all alone. I hope this book gives you a framework in which you can act in ways that inspire others to follow your vision and passion. Movements are not built alone—they require collaboration and the effort of many types of people. Because women are great relationship builders, this should come fairly easily. But because of our tendency to do it all alone, we forget to reach out, ask for help, and partner up with others. By now you probably realize that there can be a different approach, one that requires a bit more vulnerability and an embracing of the potentiality of the future. Finding supportive communities of women is another great way to harness the power of women and to help each other along the way, so I strongly encourage you to find those types of communities around you because they are there. And if you can't find one near you, start one! Chances are there are like-minded women who are up to big things just like you and would love the support and encouragement.

For the aspiring or active change-makers out there who have tried any of the above, you know how challenging it can be to do so while living in the current paradigm. Just turn on the news, and any optimism for change or transformation rapidly dissipates. It therefore becomes even more critical to be aware of your own state of mind and state of inner well-being. From personal experience, I know that the best way to do this is by learning how to nurture a positive mental state, connecting with like-minded people, staying motivated and inspired, and working collaboratively with others towards a common goal. Uplifting others is a sure way to staying uplifted yourself. When we can maintain this positive mind-set, we can increase our ability to manifest our desired future by tenfold. The Law of Attraction, the Secret, whatever you want to call it, does work! And women have a powerful ability to manifest their desired outcomes when they stand in their true feminine power. That is why I believe women can and will change the world— by being pioneers and trailblazing these types of collaborative processes in systems that need transformation.

It's the Small Acts that Lead to Change

I also want to point out that you don't necessarily have to have a big mission or vision in order to make an impact in the world. Sometimes we think we need to do big things in order to create change. But who is to say that the smaller actions—smiling at a stranger, giving money to a homeless person, or taking care of an ailing grandparent, aren't just as meaningful or impactful? Staying open-hearted, doing acts of generosity, giving selflessly and nurturing are all feminine qualities. Although they not directly part of the FLM, they are just as important and deserve to be mentioned here. When we approach people and situations from a place of love, from a place of total openness and connection, it can be a powerful act. As we allow our technology to take away opportunities for intimacy and true connection, we starve ourselves of this basic human need. So let's not forget how important it is for our individual well-being and for the well-being of others, and let's find ways to meaningfully connect with others on a regular basis. It's part of the notion of self-care, and an integral step in nurturing our inner world so we can tap into our true potential.

Another step you can take in supporting yourself on your journey is to connect with other women in this work. Research shows that when there is not a critical mass for a new behavior, women tend to go back to the status quo. Showing up as an empowered, feminine and balanced leader might be lonely at first. But the more you become a role model and advocate by simply embracing these qualities and leveraging them in your everyday approach, the more you can pave the way for others to do the same. Have conversations about this with your colleagues or teammates, or bring it up regularly with the women on your team. Encourage them to think about their leadership style and the impact they are making. If you are in a position of influence inside your company, think about investing in this work through training, coaching, and other development opportunities. Engage in conversations with men as well—get their feedback on these issues and see how they react. It's imperative that we get men on board to support gender equality; if we are to close the gap, we need more men advocating on behalf of women.

Once we do the work required on ourselves to stand fully in our power, we can then invite men to do the same. However, if we approach them from the old paradigm—from a place of weakness or victimhood or even blame (as I see happening more frequently), it will be very difficult to gain men as allies. Angry feminists, who like to laugh at men and belittle them when they are trying to support women in areas like tech, are only doing a disservice to women as a whole. Engaging in deep dialogue is another powerful way we can begin shifting biases and stereotypes toward more equality and understanding between the sexes.

Money Talks

Another area I'd like to address is women's willingness (or the lack thereof) to invest in themselves and in other women. This is a controversial topic because we see lots of money being invested in women's development by companies through diversity and inclusion initiatives, so it's hard to say this isn't happening. But through my personal experience I have seen a genuine lack of willingness by women to develop the necessary skills to be better leaders, managers, or entrepreneurs when it comes to having to pay for it themselves.

I see the same behavior by women when it comes to investing in women-led companies, or supporting women-led ventures. This "scarcity" mentality, as I like to call it, goes back to a lack of confidence, lack of worthiness, and not valuing ourselves. We have to do better when it comes to investing in our development and demanding that companies do a better job as well. And through our collective action, we can convince venture capital firms to start investing in women-led companies to level the uneven playing field that exists at the moment. In fact, only 2.7% of companies that received venture capital funding between 2011 and 2013 had a woman CEO, according to a recent study. And today, only 36% of U.S. business owners are women, according to the Small Business Administration.

So how do we change these numbers? The first step is for women to not hold themselves back from even just attempting to start a company or applying for funding and believing in their ideas and abilities. Next is to embrace our feminine leadership more fully and build the right relationships and, using the FLM, build the right relationships and partnerships that will get us there. And the third is to create more opportunities for women to invest in each other, like Plum Alley, a crowd-funding platform for woman-led businesses, and Pink51, an online marketplace for women led businesses. And let's not judge these types of platforms as weak or biased—women helping other women is a necessary and powerful action that creates more opportunities for women to bring their visions to life, and having dedicated places where this is promoted and encouraged is a great step in leveling the playing field.

Next Steps and Accountability

By now, if you've done the exercises in this book and applied the tools to how you lead and manage others, you should be noticing some changes. What is shifting for you? How are you relating to others differently? Are you receiving any feedback or input? Begin to pay attention to the people and the situations you find yourself in, and be aware of the impact you're making. Don't expect everything to be perfect, because chances are they won't be. This stuff takes practice; it takes a willingness to fail and learn from your mistakes and to begin again. Every great leader has the capacity to fail, but to fail quickly and to get back up, brush themselves off, and adjust accordingly. This type of resilience is something women must learn to do if they are to succeed, and this is a great time for them to start building that muscle.

Nothing that is worth doing is easy, but the results you can expect if you stick with it will be worth it in the end. It takes constant awareness, persistence, and some getting used to, but we all have the capacity to change our behavior if we start by changing how we think and what we believe. The framework and exercises in this book are designed to help you do just that. However, if you find yourself struggling, you may want to go back and re-read some chapters, spend more time in reflection, or think about hiring a coach that can help you develop these skill sets through more customized and individualized guidance. Asking for feedback from others is a great way to gauge your progress as well, and I would even encourage you to tell your superiors or colleagues that you're working on developing these skills. That way they can participate in helping your development through honest feedback, which can often times be invaluable in helping us get to that next level.

Another important step in working toward change is creating accountability by setting realistic and attainable goals for yourself. Make sure you set yourself up for success by setting goals that are reachable, and create structures that help you get there. One way of doing that is asking a friend to hold you accountable, or working on these skills with someone else and creating a buddy system of accountability. I always recommend focusing on a few key areas to improve that will make the most impact in your leadership style. You can create a Mastermind group where you work on these concepts and hold each other accountable that way. Find whatever works for you, but set goals that are realistic and set them where you have accountability to yourself and others. And make sure you celebrate your successes along the way!

Keeping the Conversations Going

In order to stay in the conversation about this topic of Feminine Leadership, I'd like to invite you to keep the momentum going by offering a few ways to stay connected. You can visit www.moniquetallon.com for links to an exclusive Facebook Community group that will be available for readers of this book. Here you'll find access to other like-minded women where you can connect, learn and support other women on their Feminine Leadership journey. You can also sign up for our newsletter that will announce any events, workshops or programs I will be offering to all of you, including individual coaching and on-going professional development courses. So make sure to visit www.moniquetallon.com to stay connected and continue the learning!

A Vision for a New World

I'll leave you with this thought—how would you like to live in a world led by more women? I believe there is a real yearning for things to be different, for more balance in the world through embodiment of the feminine. I believe that deep down inside, we all want to live in a more just and equitable society where things like empathy, compassion, nurturing, and connection are valued and cherished. A world where people are genuinely heard, listened to, and respected. A world where people, not corporations, are valued. Where the planet is considered in all the business decisions that are made. A place where violence and senseless murder are no longer the norm. We are all aching to create a more beautiful world that our hearts know is possible.

In order to achieve this, we need a critical mass of truly empowered and balanced women to lead the change along with men. Feminine leaders have great vision and through their compelling message, inspire and act in a collaborative way. They are willing to be vulnerable, and practice empathy. They can also be decisive and assertive when needed, tapping into their intuition for guidance. They can be caring for themselves and others. They are resilient and humble. We need more women who are graceful leaders, embodying these important qualities by being willing to go out of their comfort zone and reach for positions of power where decisions impacting the masses are made. We need women to continue to stand up and have the courage to speak out in the face of injustice. And most importantly, we need women to speak up and pursue their gifts and express themselves in whatever way brings them joy.

But change starts with yourself. Hopefully the exercises and guidance in the book will help you on that journey. You can also be part of the movement by spreading the word, sharing this book and these concepts with your friends, colleagues, teammates, and supervisors, men and women alike. Engage in active dialogue and be the change you want to see in the world. It may not happen today, it might not happen tomorrow, but there will come a day when women are more equally represented in the leadership arena. It's up to all of us to take personal responsibility by working on ourselves to bring that change into reality. How will *you* become a game-changer?

Resources

Here is a list of resources I've mentioned in the book as well as additional links to books and sites that could be useful in your leadership development.

Books:

- Nonviolent Communication by Marshall Rosenberg, Ph.D.
- The Confidence Code by Katty Kay & Claire Shipman
- The Athena Doctrine by John Gerzema & Michael D'Antonio
- The Gifts of Imperfection by Brené Brown
- Thrive by Arianna Huffington
- Anatomy of Peace by The Arbinger Institute

Ted Talks:

- The Power of Vulnerability by Brené Brown
- The Athena Doctrine by John Gerzema
- The Power of Introverts by Susan Cain

Women-led for Women Ventures:

- Plum Alley: A Crowdfunding Platform for Women-Led Businesses
- Pink 51: A marketplace of women led businesses
- The Coaching Fellowship: Pro-bono coaching fellowship for young female social entrepreneurs
- Golden Seeds: An early-stage angel investment group with a focus on women leaders

Acknowledgments

I am the great-granddaughter of a survivor of the Armenian genocide. My great-grandmother, Maritza Asdourian, witnessed the killing of almost her entire family and was deported into the Syrian desert of Deir ez-Zhor along with two of her young children. As she awaited certain death, after burying one of her children and almost committing suicide from despair, she had an intuition that she might possibly escape. Overhearing a plan by a group of men who were trying to escape at night, she convinced them to take her along, regardless of the fact that she had a child that would slow them down. Through courage, faith, and belief in herself, she was able to walk through the desert and find refuge in Aleppo, Syria, where she ended up settling, remarrying, and having another child, my grandmother Lucine.

Although I never had the privilege of meeting Maritza, I did have the honor of growing up with her stories of perseverance, and her strength and courage will live on in me forever.

When I was faced with my greatest fear of climbing the 40-foot tree, I silently thanked her when I made it to the top because I knew she had been with me at that moment. The power that surged within my belly, the inner knowing of how to climb the tree, and the courage that got me to the top reminded me of my great-grandmother's strength. I will be forever grateful to her for embodying the meaning of true feminine power and showing me the way.

I want to thank my former coworker Jenny Morrow for being the kind of supportive mentor and manager that all women should have, and for introducing me to Kim Dusel McGuire, who introduced me to The Coaches Training Institute (CTI) where I discovered the art and profession of coaching. The many teachers I had at CTI, including Susan Carlisle, whose wisdom and expertise inspired me to become a coach, and to Henry and Karen Kimsey-House for their great leadership and vision behind CTI. I want to thank Art Shirk, Caroline Hall, and the Raccoon tribe, for helping me get up the tree and find my inner power and for teaching me how compelling it is to be authentic. I want to thank Wendy Palmer for teaching me about Leadership Embodiment and how we can harness our inner power through the body. Special thanks goes to my coach and mentor, Valerie Ryder, who has encouraged and guided me the whole way and was one of the first people to urge me to write. Special thanks to Bob Douglas and Delano Amiel for the many hours of editing that went into making this manuscript grammatically correct, consistent and just that much better.

I also want to thank my wonderful husband Chris, whose unending love and support healed the hole in my heart, made me trust the universe again, and was my rock and a source of much encouragement during the writing of this book.

Special thanks to my family—my mom Anahit, my father Gerard, and my sister Rosy. The roles you have played in my life have helped me grow into the person I am today, and for that I will be eternally grateful. And a special thanks to my cousin Victoria, who has continuously believed in my writing and has been a support throughout my life.

Thank you to the women who let me feature their stories in my book, including Julie Thorne Engles, Susan Petoyan, Rosie Cofre, Diane Reichenberger, and others.

Many thanks to the many women who have fought the hard battles that have won us the rights we enjoy today. Thanks to the men and women who continue to fight for equal pay, for a woman's right to choose, for gay rights, civil rights, and the rights of the planet and of all human beings. May you continue to step into your power to co-create a better world.

Notes

9   **third women's revolution:** Arianna Huffington, Thrive – The Third Metric to Redefining Success and Creating a Life of WellBeing, Wisdom & Wonder (New York: Harmony Books, 2014), 23.

12   **And only 21:** Catalyst. "Women CEOs of the S&P 500." New York: Catalyst, November 18, 2015. http://www.catalyst.org/knowledge/women-ceos-sp-500.

12   **Of 197 heads:** Valbona Zeneli, "Women's Rights Are Human Rights," The Globalist March 8, 2014, http://www.theglobalist.com/10-facts-international-womens-day/.

12   **In national politics:** Center for American Women and Politics (CAWP). Eagleton Institute of Politics. Rutgers, State University of New Jersey, Fact Sheet: "Women in the U.S. Congress," 2015, http://www.cawp.rutgers.edu/current-numbers.

12   **For women of:** Center for American Women and Politics (CAWP). Eagleton Institute of Politics. Rutgers, State University of New Jersey, Fact Sheet: "Women of Color in

185

Elective Office," 2015, http://www.cawp.rutgers.edu/ women-color-elective-office-2015.

12 **In 2014, women:** Institute for Women's Policy Research. "About Pay Equity and Discrimination," http://www.iwpr.org/ initiatives/pay-equity-and-discrimination.

12 **outperformed those with the least by 66 percent:** Catalyst Report, The Bottom Line: Corporate Performance and Women's Representation on Boards (2007).

12 **to make sound decisions:** "Women Make Better Decisions Than Men," e-Science News.com, March 26, 2013. http:// esciencenews.com/articles/2013/03/26/women.make.better. decisions.men.

13 **social enterprises being led by women:** "State of Social Enterprise Survey," (2014), http://www.socialenterprise.org.uk/ uploads/files/2013/07/the_peoples_business.pdf.

13 **generous when there is a woman present:** Adam Grant, "Why Men Need Women," The New York Times, July 20, 2013, http://www.nytimes.com/2013/07/21/opinion/sunday/ whymen-need-women.html?pagewanted=all&_r=2&.

13 **she was a:** Andy Serwer, "Carly Fiorina's record at HewlettPackard, by the numbers," Yahoo Finance, April 29, 2015, http://finance.yahoo.com/news/carly-fiorina-s-record-athewlett-packard—by-the-numbers-184234108.html.

16 **positively impact organizational performance:** Alice H Eagly, Johannesen-Schmidt, and Van Engen, Transformational, Transactional & Laissez-Faire Leadership Styles, (2003).

18 **according to Wikipedia:** https://en.wikipedia.org/wiki/ Feminism.

CHAPTER 2: *Redefining the Relationship With Ourselves*

25   **This power center:** Kelli Jo Conn, "The Seven Chakras," Updated December 21, 2015, http://healing.about.com/od/chakratheseven/a/study7chakras.htm.

CHAPTER 3: *Masculine vs. Feminine Leadership Styles*

33   **According to a recent study:** Alice H. Eagly and Linda L. Carli. Women & the Labyrinth of Leadership. Harvard Business Review. September, (2007).

38   **In a study done by the University of Pennsylvania:** Catherine Paddock, Ph.D., "Brain Wired Differently in Men and Women," December 4, 2013, http://www.medicalnewstoday.com/articles/269652.php.

39   **not set and can change throughout life:** "Men and Women's Brain Wired Differently," BBC News, December 3, 2013, http://www.bbc.com/news/health-25198063.

41   **men thought more like women:** John Gerzema and Michael D'Antonio. The Athena Doctrine. (San Francisco: Jossey-Bass, 2013).

49   **In a recent Gallop poll survey:** Rebecca Riffkin, "Americans still prefer a male boss to a female boss," October 14, 2014, http://www.gallup.com/poll/178484/americans-prefer-maleboss-female-boss.aspx.

CHAPTER 4: *Vision*

59   **In fact, according to:** Alice H. Eagly and Linda L. Carli. Women & the Labyrinth of Leadership. Harvard Business Review. September, (2007).

64 **people still associate:** Alice H. Eagly and Linda L. Carli. Women & the Labyrinth of Leadership. Harvard Business Review. September, (2007).

CHAPTER 5: *Vulnerability*

72   **Women no longer:** Stevenson & Wolfers, The Paradox of
     Declining Female Happiness (Cambridge: National Bureau of
     Economic Research, 2009).

76   **In the words of one female leader:** Alice H. Eagly and Linda
     L. Carli. Women & the Labyrinth of Leadership. Harvard
     Business Review. September, (2007).

CHAPTER 6: *Care*

82   **have to work approximately 60 extra days:** Eileen Patten,
     "On Equal Pay Day, key facts about the gender gap," April 14,
     2015, http://www.pewresearch.org/fact-tank/2014/04/08/ on-
     equal-pay-day-everything-you-need-to-know-about-thegender-
     pay-gap/.

82   **In comparison, men:** Larissa Faw, "Why Millennial Women
     Are Burning Out At Work by 30," Forbes, November 11, 2011,
     http://www.forbes.com/sites/larissafaw/2011/11/11/ why-
     millennial-women-are-burning-out-at-work-by-30/.

84   **Ann Marie Slaughter points this out: Ann Marie Slaughter,
     "Why Wome**n Still Can't Have it All," The Atlantic, July/
     August 2012 issue, http://www.theatlantic.com/magazine/
     archive/2012/07/why-women-still-cant-have-it-all/309020/.

93   **coaching and mentoring others:** Transformational,
     Transactional & Laissez-Faire Leadership Styles, Alice H Eagly,
     Mary C Johannesen-Schmidt and Marloes L.Van Engen, 2003;

     McKinsey survey and analysis, 2008; The Leadership
     Styles of Women and Men, Alice H Eagly and Mary C
     JohannesenSchmidt, 2001.

CHAPTER 7: *Intuition*

98   **ground-breaking book:** Louann Brizendine, MD, The Female
     Brain (New York: Broadway Books, 2006), 120-121.

106 **compared to 29% of girls:** Suzanne Daley, "Little Girls Lose their Self-Esteem Way to Adolescence, Study Finds," New York Times, January 9, 1991, http://www.nytimes.com/1991/01/09/education/little-girls-lose-their-self-esteem-way-to-adolescencestudy-finds.html.

106 **The natural result:** Katty Kay and Claire Shipman, "The Confidence Gap," The Atlantic, May 2014 issue, http:// www.theatlantic.com/magazine/archive/2014/05/ the-confidence-gap/359815/.

107 **stuff that turns thoughts into action:** Katty Kay and Claire Shipman, "The Confidence Gap," The Atlantic, May 2014 issue, http://www.theatlantic.com/magazine/archive/2014/05/the-confidence-gap/359815/.

108 **think we are beautiful:** Katty Kay and Claire Shipman, The Confidence Code, (New York: Harper Collins, 2014), 99.

CHAPTER 8: *Empathy*

115 **think of leading and learning:** Joshua Freedman, "The Neuroscience of learning and leading," Forbes, May 8, 2013, http://www.forbes.com/sites/ashoka/2013/05/08/ the-neuroscience-at-the-heart-of-learning-and-leading/.

115 **academic performance as well:** "A Case for Emotional Intelligence in our Schools," November 2, 2007, http:// www.6seconds.org/2007/11/02/a-case-for-emotional-intelligence-in-our-schools/.

115 **also make more money:** "A Case for Emotional Intelligence in our Schools," November 2, 2007, http://www.6seconds.org/ case/leadership-and-emotional-intelligence/.

115 **pays to care, widely and deeply:** Joshua Freedman, "The Neuroscience of learning and leading," Forbes, May 8, 2013, http://www.forbes.com/sites/ashoka/2013/05/08/ the-neuroscience-at-the-heart-of-learning-and-leading/.

119 **List of Universal Human Needs and Values:** Center for Nonviolent Communication, 2005, http://www.cnvc.org.

129 **many facets of civil society:** http://www. livingroomconversations.org/about/.

CHAPTER 9: *Collaboration*

149 **In 2000, Ilaria:** https://www.youtube.com/ watch?v=hIesZXYH4X0.

CHAPTER 10: *Humility*

160 **reasons women opt out:** Catherine Ashcraft, Ph.D. and Sarah Blithe. Women in IT: The Facts. National Center for Women & Information Technology (2009, 2010), http://www.ncwit.org/ sites/default/files/legacy/pdf/NCWIT_TheFacts_rev2010.pdf.

CHAPTER 11: *Become a Game-Changer*

169 16 million children: Wight, Chau, and Aratani. "Who are America's Poor Children? The Official Story," 2010, http://*www. nccp.org/ topics/ childpoverty.html.*

173 **only 2.7% of companies:** Associated Press, "Study on Funding Reveals Massive Gender Discrepancies," http://www.inc.com/ associated-press/women-led-businesses-get-little-venture-capital. html.

173 **according to the Small Business Administration:** Associated Press, "Study on Funding Reveals Massive Gender Discrepancies," http://www.inc.com/kimberly-weisul/whereare-the-best-countries-for-women-entrepreneurs.html